To Jess, my true love and best friend.

ac4d

Austin Center for Design
PO Box 11572, Austin Texas 78711

© 2012 Jon Kolko; licensed under a Creative Commons Attribution-NonCommercial-ShareAlike 3.0 Unported License. This license means that, while the author retains the copyright to the work, you are permitted to:

- Share this work with anyone you like, as long as you don't charge money for it

- Change this work and re-release it under your own name, with attribution to the original source

- Integrate this work into your own work in small or large portions

Notices

To the fullest extent of the law, neither the Publisher nor the authors, contributors, or editors, assume any liability for any injury and/or damage to persons or property as a matter of products liability, negligence, or otherwise, or from any use or operation of any methods, products, instructions, or ideas contained in the material herein.

ISBN: 978-0-6155931-5-9

For information on this publication or to read it online, visit our website at www.wickedproblems.com

For information about Austin Center for Design, visit our website at www.ac4d.com

Production Credits

Writing: Jon Kolko

Editing: Ronnie Lipton

Contributed Content: Ruby Ku, Ryan Hubbard, Kat Davis, Christina Tran, Chap Ambrose, Scott Magee, Alex Pappas

Cover Photograpy: Chap Ambrose

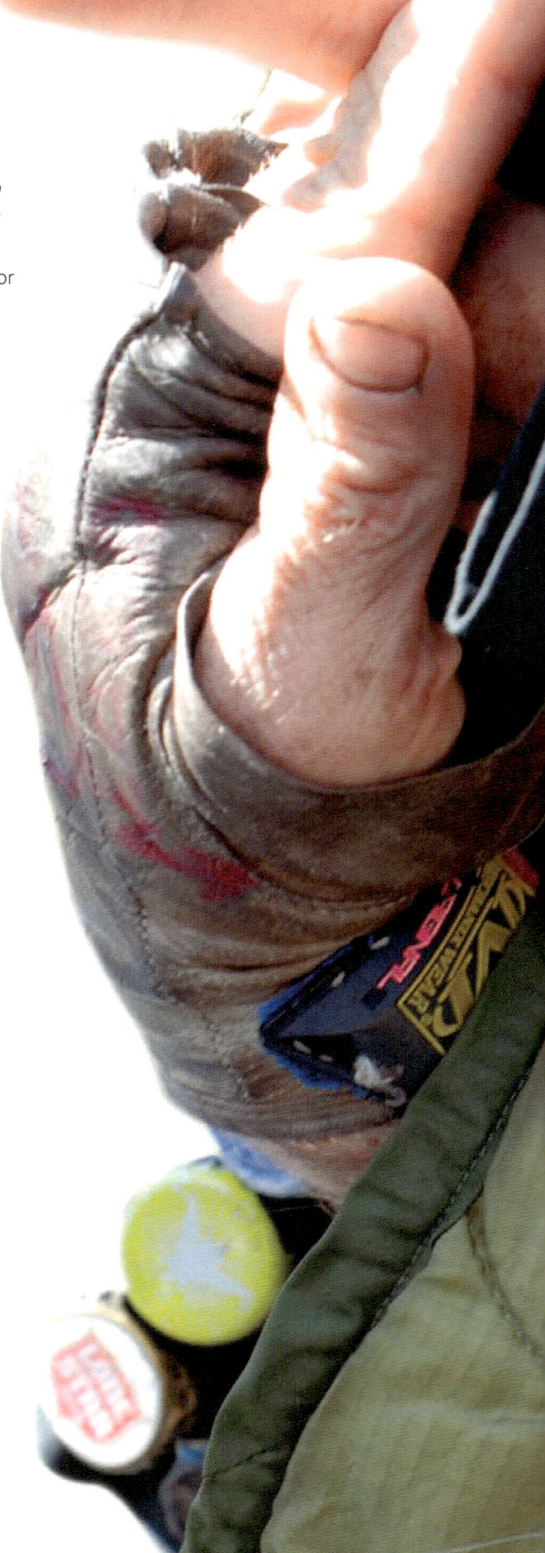

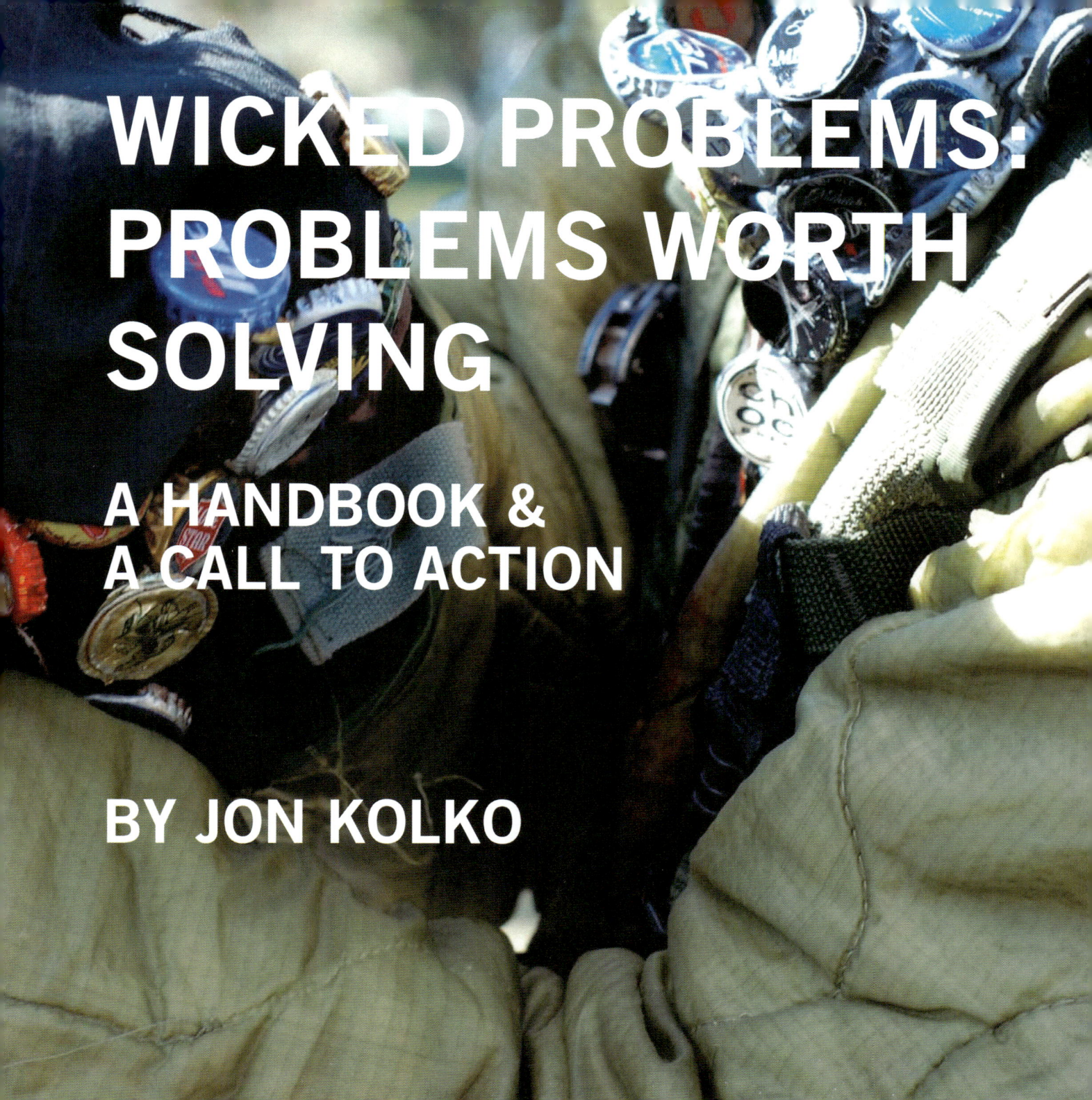

WICKED PROBLEMS: PROBLEMS WORTH SOLVING

A HANDBOOK & A CALL TO ACTION

BY JON KOLKO

CONTENTS

Section One
An Introduction to Wicked Problems — 4

My Epiphany	6
Understanding Social Entrepreneurship	8
Wicked Problems	10
A Large-Scale Distraction	12
A Changing Workforce	21
Alex Pappas, On Inspiration	24
Existing Approaches to Social Entrepreneurship	26
Short Project, Shallow Focus	28
Ryan Hubbard, On Impact	34
A Designerly Approach to Social Entrepreneurship	36

Section Two
Skills for the Social Entrepreneur — 40

Building Empathy by Designing With	42
Kat Davis, On Empathy	48
Cultural Sensitivity	50
Informed Inferences Through Synthesis	55
Ruby Ku, On Money	59
Public Making	60
Christina Tran, On Momentum and Focus	68

Section Three
Teaching and Learning — 70

Common Models of Design Education	72
A Curriculum Template	76

Section Four
Methods — 98

Methods for Conducting Research and Gaining Empathy

Contextual Inquiry	100
Applied: Pocket Hotline	103
Participatory Design	105
Cultural Probes	106

Methods for Synthesizing Data and Developing Ideas

2x2	108
Theory of Change	110
Applied: HourSchool	116
Concept Mapping	118
Semantic Zoom	122
Insight Combination	126

Methods for Creating New Designs

Scenario Planning	128
Use Cases	132
Storyboard	136
Journey Map	140
Bodystorming	144
Service Blueprint	146

Methods for Planning a Business

Revenue and Expense Worksheet	150
Triple-Tiered Subsidy Worksheet	154
Product and Feature Roadmap	158

Conclusion   162

AN INTRODUCTION TO WICKED PROBLEMS

This section first introduces the idea of wicked problems—large-scale social issues that plague humanity, like poverty or malnutrition—and then describes the role of design in mitigating these problems.

MY EPIPHANY

I became interested in the power of design in social contexts during a project at my former employer, frog design. Project Masiluleke (or Project M) was organized by Pop!Tech, frog, and MTN, an African mobile phone operator. Project M was designed to help stop the spread of AIDS in KwaZulu-Natal, a South African province with about 10 million people, including an estimated four million who are HIV-positive and 400,000 who will develop AIDS *each year*.[1] In many ways, the societal norms of the country were more difficult to overcome than lack of test kit accessibility, the interdisciplinary team routinely noticed during initial research. During an interview, one resident explained, "I don't want people to see me standing in queues. I want it to be private and secret." Another said, "I wouldn't visit the clinic because of the undignified way health care workers handle the issues of patients." A third explained, "People are so afraid to go to the clinic." Because complex issues of privacy, sexual identity, and fear stood in the way of desired, healthy behavior, the solution needed to address them along with the biological spread of the disease.

Research also showed that an estimated 80% to 90% of South Africans have access to a mobile phone. So the designers developed a system that uses mobile messaging channels to raise awareness of the disease and directly link to HIV counseling and other support services. The designers embedded health care messages in "Please Call Me" messages (PCMs), a type of free messaging in Europe and Africa that is used primarily in poor communities. These PCMs arrived discreetly on personal phones.

In the first three days of Project M's message distribution, the National AIDS Helpline received 5,000 calls a day, *three times* its usual number.[2]

After frog launched Project M, I started wondering why more of our work wasn't focused on efforts like this; this was just one small project in a sea of otherwise standard, traditional design work. I quickly came to realize that, despite the well-intentions of

---

1 Dugger, Celia. "South Africa Is Seen to Lag in H.I.V. Fight." July 20, 2009. http://www.nytimes.com/2009/07/20/world/africa/20circumcision.html (accessed October 1, 2011). Only 500,000 people have been tested for the disease and know their status, and of the 200,000 people in treatment, close to 40% will abandon the treatment program within two years.

2 Yale School of Management. Project Masiluleke: Texting and Testing to Fight HIV/AIDS in South Africa. n.d. http://nexus.som.yale.edu/design-project-m/ (Accessed November 14, 2011)

nearly everyone at the company, and despite the large-scale positive evidence that the work was actually doing what it was supposed to, and despite the massive and positive PR the company received, it was a simple question of economics. frog—owned by a company named Aricent, which in turn is owned by a "leading global investment firm with deep roots in private equity", is expected to produce a certain amount of money every quarter. Project M wasn't making money, and while it wasn't losing money either, it simply didn't compare to the profitability of a large corporate engagement.

This begs the question: if, at an extremely creative, well intentioned, and supportive company, Project M is the exception and not the norm, how can this type of work possibly have a chance?

I think the answer is in social entrepreneurship.

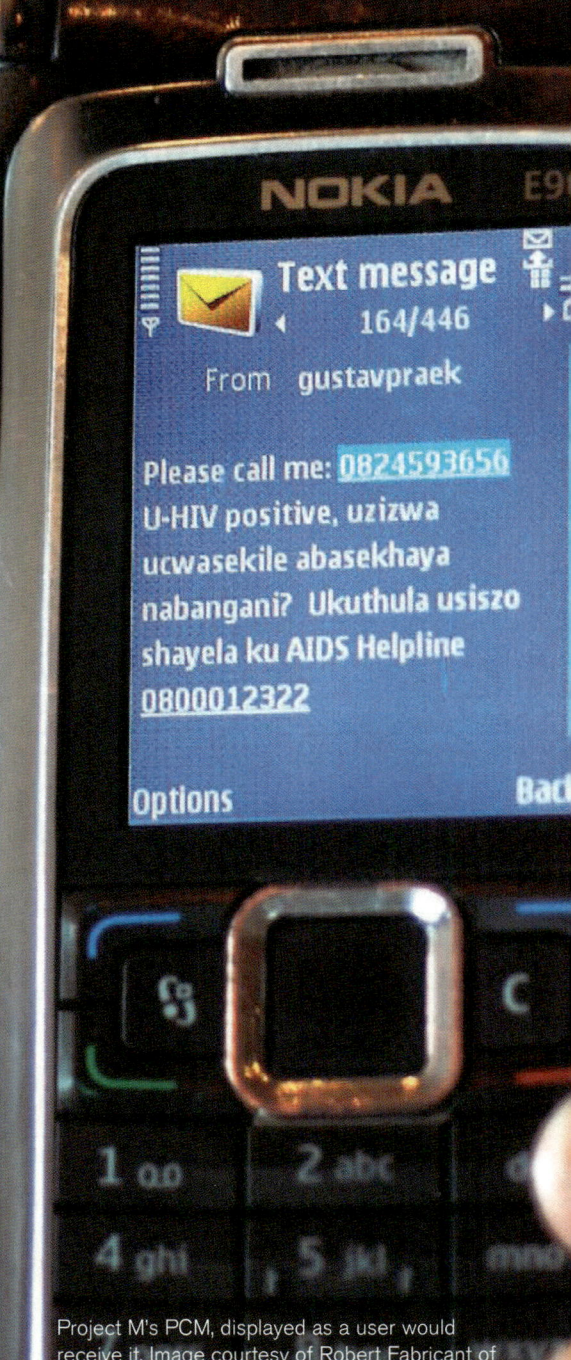

Project M's PCM, displayed as a user would receive it. Image courtesy of Robert Fabricant of frog design.

UNDERSTANDING SOCIAL ENTREPRENEURSHIP

Entrepreneurship is at the heart of Western culture. For many people, it invokes feelings of freedom and liberty. Many people also find it a tremendously intimidating idea—one that implies a Renaissance-style mastery of anything and everything. But that's an inflated impression created by the lore of entrepreneurship and the framing of American history. An entrepreneur in practice is simply someone who starts a company, assumes the financial risk—*and* benefits from the reward.

An entrepreneur is often driven by awareness of a problem and a passion to solve that problem. James Dyson, inventor of the Dyson vacuum cleaner, is said to have become so irritated by the lack of suction in the standard vacuum cleaner that he dedicated his life to building a better version. "5 years and 5,127 prototypes later, the world's first bagless vacuum cleaner from Dyson arrived," [3] and Dyson's net worth is now about a billion dollars. [4]

Like an entrepreneur, a social entrepreneur starts a company and assumes the risk. The difference, though, is the type of problem. A social entrepreneur works in the context of a humanitarian problem. Rather than efforts directed toward something like better vacuuming (and large economic profits), the drive is toward helping people and creating *social capital*, the non-economic wealth within a community.

According to Author Jane Jacobs, the diverse mesh of human knowledge and relationships in cities are networks, and "these networks are a city's irreplaceable social capital." [5] Sociologists theorize over the relationship between social capital and quality of life, and "many now regard social capital as a key ingredient in both economic development and stable liberal democracy." [6]

Social entrepreneurs notice pressing problems—that often include inequality, education, access to food and water, and sustainability—and seek to solve them. Like Dyson, social entrepreneurs rigorously create prototypes. The prototype and output can be physical, as in a mosquito net

---

3 Dyson. "A New Idea." n.d. http://www.dyson.com/about/story/default.asp?searchType=story&story=newidea (accessed October 2011).

4 Clark, Hannah. "James Dyson Cleans Up." August 1, 2006. http://www.forbes.com/2006/08/01/leadership-facetime-dyson-cx_hc_0801dyson.html (accessed October 24, 2011).

5 Jacobs, Jane. The Death and Life of Great American Cities. 1961.

6 Fukuyama, Francis. "Social Capital and Development: The Coming Agenda." SAIS Review, 2002: 23-37.

to prevent malaria or a testing kit to reduce the spread of HIV. Or they can be digital, the result of the complexity of social problems, the cheap cost of technology, and the ability to easily distribute a piece of software across large distances.

The design of an object, such as a mosquito net, or an interaction, as in Project M, is often part of a larger framework—a *service*—that also includes people and policies.

As a social entrepreneur, Dr. Govindappa Venkataswamy understood the social-capital potential of a country less afflicted by blindness. So he founded Aravind Eye Hospital to provide free eye care to the millions of Indians suffering from treatable blindness.

In this case, the service is made up of various artifacts (such as forms to fill out, waiting-room chairs), interactions (the systems that track the number of patients and their days in the hospital), people (doctors, nurses, patients, case workers, etc.), and policies (governing the hospital's operation). [7]

When all of these elements act in concert, Aravind is most effective at achieving its mission, creating the maximum social capital, and tackling something called a *wicked problem*.

---

7 Pavithra Mehta, Suchitra Shenoy. Infinite Vision. CharityFocus, 2011.

WICKED PROBLEMS

A wicked problem is a social or cultural problem that is difficult or impossible to solve for as many as four reasons: incomplete or contradictory knowledge, the number of people and opinions involved, the large economic burden, and the interconnected nature of these problems with *other* problems. Poverty is linked with education, nutrition with poverty, the economy with nutrition, and so on. These problems are typically offloaded to policy makers, or are written off as being too cumbersome to handle en masse. Yet these are the problems—poverty, sustainability, equality, and health and wellness—that plague our cities and our world and that touch each and every one of us. These problems can be mitigated through the process of design, which is an intellectual approach that emphasizes empathy, abductive reasoning, and rapid prototyping.

Horst Rittel, one of the first to formalize a theory of wicked problems, cites ten characteristics of these complicated social issues:

1. Wicked problems have no definitive formulation. The problem of poverty in Texas is grossly similar but discretely different from poverty in Nairobi, so no practical characteristics describe "poverty."
2. It's hard, maybe impossible, to measure or claim success with wicked problems because they bleed into one another, unlike the boundaries of traditional design problems that can be articulated or defined.
3. Solutions to wicked problems can be only good or bad, not true or false. There is no idealized end state to arrive at, and so approaches to wicked problems should be tractable ways to *improve* a situation rather than solve it.
4. There is no template to follow when tackling a wicked problem, although history may provide a guide. Teams that approach wicked problems must literally make things up as they go along.

5. There is always more than one explanation for a wicked problem, with the appropriateness of the explanation depending greatly on the individual perspective of the designer.
6. Every wicked problem is a symptom of another problem. The interconnected quality of socio-economic political systems illustrates how, for example, a change in education will cause new behavior in nutrition.
7. No mitigation strategy for a wicked problem has a definitive scientific test because humans invented wicked problems and science exists to understand natural phenomena.
8. Offering a "solution" to a wicked problem frequently is a "one shot" design effort because a significant intervention changes the design space enough to minimize the ability for trial and error.
9. Every wicked problem is unique.
10. Designers attempting to address a wicked problem must be fully responsible for their actions. [8]

Based on these characteristics, not all hard-to-solve problems are wicked, only those with an indeterminate scope and scale. So most *social* problems—such as inequality, political instability, death, disease, or famine—*are* wicked. They can't be "fixed." But because of the role of design in developing infrastructure, designers can play a central role in mitigating the negative consequences of wicked problems and positioning the broad trajectory of culture in new and more desirable directions. This mitigation is not an easy, quick, or solitary exercise. While traditional circles of entrepreneurship focus on speed and agility, designing for impact is about staying the course through methodical, rigorous iteration. Due to the system qualities of these large problems, knowledge of science, economics, statistics, technology, medicine, politics, and more are necessary for effective change. This demands interdisciplinary collaboration, and most importantly, perseverance.

---

[8] Rittel, Horst. "Dilemmas in a General Theory of Planning." Policy Sciences, 1973: 155-169.

A LARGE-SCALE DISTRACTION

Why don't we already focus our efforts on wicked problems? It seems that our powerful companies and consultancies have become distracted by a different type of problem: *differentiation*. Innovation describes some form of differentiation or newness. But in product design and product development, tiered releases and *differentiation* often replace innovation, although they often are claimed as such. Consider the automotive industry, where vehicles in an existing brand are introduced each year with only subtle aesthetic or feature changes. For example, except for slight interior changes and a few new safety features, the 2012 Ford F-150 is the same as the vehicle offered the year before. [9] This phenomenon also is true of other industries, such as toys, appliances, consumer electronics, fashion, even foods, beverages, and services.

This idea of constant but meaningless change drives a machine of consumption, where advertisers pressure those with extra purchasing power into unnecessary upgrades through a fear of being left behind. Consultants and product managers craft product roadmaps that describe the progressive qualities of incremental changes. In fact, it's considered a best practice and a standard operating procedure to launch subsequent releases of the same product—with minor cosmetic changes—in subsequent months after the original product's launch. For example, between its 1990 launch and the end of 2004, Canon released 11 versions of its Rebel camera (in 1990, 1992, 1993, 1996, 1999, February and September of 2002, March and September of 2003, April and September of 2004). [10] And Apple has released a new version of the iPod every year since its 2001 launch. [11]

---

9 Ford. F150 Detailed Comparison. n.d. http://www.ford.com/trucks/f150/compare/?vehicles=30211|32979|31007|29694 (accessed November 14, 2011).

10 Wikipedia. Canon EOS. n.d. https://secure.wikimedia.org/wikipedia/en/wiki/Canon_EOS (accessed November 11, 2011).

11 Wikipedia. iPod. n.d. https://secure.wikimedia.org/wikipedia/en/wiki/IPod (accessed November 11, 2011).

This constant push is characterized as a "release cycle"—the amount of time between versions of a product reaching the market. For most of industrialized history, a release cycle for a product was a year or more; complicated offerings like vehicles typically took three or more years from product conception to launch. But technology has afforded advances not only in our products but in the way we *make* them, so the release cycle has shrunk—a lot. Advances in tooling and manufacturing, the influx of cheap and generic pre-made components, and the ability for software-based firmware upgrades have accelerated product release cycles to three to six months.

Tooling ensures only incremental design change. It describes the process of creating individual, giant machines that will cut, grind, injection-mold, and robotically create a particular product. The tools used to produce an Apple computer are unique to (and probably owned by) Apple, and their production is one of the most expensive parts of the product development process. For example, a simple, small die-cast tool to produce 50,000 low-quality aluminum objects may cost $25,000. It's in the company's best interest to use the tool as many times as possible before it begins to fall apart, so the tool begins to act as a design constraint for future product releases. Put another way, if our tool was designed to produce 50,000 objects, and we've only made and sold 25,000, it makes financial sense for the next version of our product to use the same tool.

Original Equipment Manufacturing (OEM) contributes to the increased speed of product cycles and is another deterrent to quality and innovation. These are generic parts that

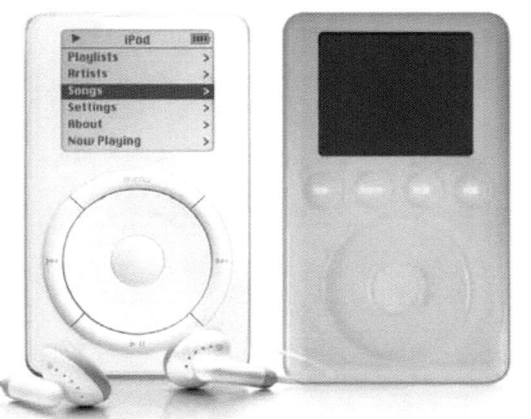

manufacturers can use rather than producing their own, decreasing the time to market by skipping the tooling process. For example, a camera company can select OEM camera bezels and internal components. After adding the logo to the sourced materials, this hypothetical company can begin shipping cameras. The company can then differentiate its OEM parts by investing time in software, adding digital features and functions to physical products to distinguish these products.

The primary driver behind incremental, mostly cosmetic innovation and a constant push of releases that leverage OEM parts is simple: **quarterly profits**. Every three months, Fortune 500 companies report their earnings to investors. If a company reports losses—or even less-than-expected gains—the price of a stock drops, investors lose money, and those with the most shares lose the most money. So stockholders want the company to make as much money as possible *in three-month increments*. And these short increments constrain any activities and initiatives that take longer than three months. Revolutionary products usually take much, much longer than three months to conceive, design, and build. Unlike a Version 3 product that can leverage an existing manufacturing plant, process, and supply and distribution chains, a new product's infrastructure must be built from scratch.

People who work at big companies try to create these revolutionary products. But each time profits are reported, the inevitable *reorganization* occurs—management's attempt to show investors increased productivity, refined or repositioned strategy, and controlled spending. This reorganization can literally move people to another area of a company or to another company altogether, and in this movement, product development initiatives are lost. Witness the early death of Microsoft Kin or HP's TouchPad—

products that internal reorganizations removed from the marketplace before they could prove their efficacy. The Kin barely lasted forty-eight days on the market [12], while TouchPad was canceled after seven weeks [13]; discussions of their death typically focus on internal fighting, misalignment with a given market strategy, cost minimization, or confusion about the products' position within the brand—rather than on the products themselves.

Ultimately, then, companies and individuals engaged in mass production are incented to drive prices down, produce the same thing over and over, innovate slowly, create differentiation in product lines only through cosmetic changes and minor feature augmentations, and *to relentlessly keep making stuff*. If we look to major brands and corporations to manage the negative consequences resulting from their work or even to drive social change and innovation, we'll be discouraged. Social change requires companies to escape the constant drive towards quarterly profits. Even those who find profitability in the social sector—and there are countless examples—require a longer iteration period than three months, so social change is destined to be ignored by the large, publicly traded corporations that possess most of the wealth and capability.

What's Wrong With Making Stuff?

At this point, a good question to ask is "what's wrong with making stuff?" After all, developed countries have worked hard to master mass-production capabilities and to increase the quality of life through conveniences and efficiencies. Designers have touched every item you own and every building you enter. And at least some of them are driven by the urge to make beautiful things that help make your life better. But design runs deeper in our culture than just the physical products we own. Design also extends to services, such as—when you go to the hospital or when you grab a burger at McDonalds. Some of these services are designed to emphasize speed and efficiency, while others are focused on more emotional goals

---

12 Helft, Miguel. "Microsoft Kin Discontinued After 48 Days." June 30, 2010. https://www.nytimes.com/2010/07/01/technology/01phone.html (accessed November 11, 2011).

13 Kumparak, Greg. "It's Official: HP Kills Off webOS Phones and the TouchPad." August 18, 2011. http://techcrunch.com/2011/08/18/its-official-hp-kills-off-webos-phones-and-the-touchpad/ (accessed November 11, 2011).

like encouraging pleasure, establishing brand value, or, in the case of the software and websites you use, making you more productive or helping you communicate with friends and family.

But although everything around you has been designed (except nature, and even that's starting to change!), **not everything has been designed well**. When we think about what good design means, we often judge the immediate features, functions, and aesthetics. Some things are ugly, or styled on a fleeting trend. Some things are hard to use or understand. Or they cost too much, perform poorly, or don't offer all the capabilities you might like.

Products are the visible and tangible output of a designer's work. Their results are easy to judge because we are immediately made aware of their consequences on our lives. We feel better, feel worse, get frustrated, accomplish our goals, talk to our friends, and so on—based on the design that helped or hindered us in our task. We can say things like "that was designed poorly because it made me miss an important meeting," or "that is designed well because it looks nice in my house."

But the less obvious results of design are the fundamental reason this book exists. These are the *consequences of design*, which tend to fall into two categories: *diffused* and *selection*.

Diffused Consequences

Cultural shifts are a direct result of individuals' work and actions, yet it feels far-fetched to give either accolades or criticism to a designer for something as broad as a culture shift. It's unlikely that a designer has considered his impact on culture (although designers do tend to have a sort of surreal experience when they first see their work on the shelf at Walmart). In fact, because culture is so abstract, large, and amorphous, few people in the world think about the impact of any individual in this way. But designers who do think about cultural impact are really thinking about *diffused* consequences: great power yielded without the ability to see direct causality from those powerful actions.

When a designer makes a product—say, a hammer—he designs all of the details of the hammer. This includes how it looks and functions, how it will be manufactured, and in many cases, how it will be packaged and appear on a shelf in a store. He probably works in his office, at a desk with a computer, surrounded by other people involved in developing the product. Before he designs his hammer, he has many conversations with engineers, marketers, and other professionals whose expertise he respects.

The designer considered the aesthetics of the hammer. He was inspired by new consumer electronics that were made of bubbly plastic, and so when he specified material, he added translucent strips to the handle, giving it a space-age feel.

Then the designer considered the shape of the hammer. He learned about human factors in college, and so he mirrored the shape of the hand to make the handle easy for people with arthritis to grasp.

And when he's finished designing the hammer, he may move on to the next product—say, a wrench set.

About three months after the hammer is designed, it rolls off the production line in a giant building in Shenzhen, China. It looks exactly how the designer specified it—each detail is "by design."

In fact, hundreds of thousands of these hammers, made exactly to specification, roll off the production line, exactly as designed.[14] Companies spend millions of dollars to optimize production and minimize manufacturing errors so that they can guarantee that the hammer at Home Depot is exactly to specification.

This designer I'm describing is a real person, and after he finished the hammer and the wrench set, he went on to design a leaf blower, a series of garden shears, large rain barrels, hose nozzles, and big plastic toolsheds for back yards. This person has had an impact on a huge number of people. If the hammer, leaf blower, and other tools are easy to use, he can claim some small part of users' happy experience with the tool. If the hammer falls apart after a few uses, he can bear some of the responsibility for the need to buy a new tool so soon after the first. And because more than 100,000 people have used this specific hammer,

---

14 My student and friend Alex Pappas designed toys that were made in China, and he describes this as the "Oh, shit" moment—where a designer realizes the scale and scope of their impact.

he'll probably have contributed to a wide variety of *consequences*—some good, some bad, but most banal. It is, after all, just a hammer.

But now think about this hammer in the larger context of all hammers, or all tools, or all products. Hundreds of kinds of hammers, toasters, cars, DVD players, socks, shoes, plastic trays, fake garden rocks, glassware, water bottles, chairs, and those little twist ties that hold your carrots together at the grocery store—they're all designed. And when you consider them—in the context of *all things that are designed*—the hammer is helping to shape culture, change behavior, and advance a set of values and priorities. Or, to be more specific, *the **designer** is shaping culture, changing behavior, and advancing his set of values and priorities*. The designer shapes trends and movements and paradigms in the slow, pervasive way that culture ebbs and flows.

Causality is when one action leads to another occurrence. It's commonly juxtaposed with association, where one action is related to another event occurring but doesn't directly cause it to happen.

Imagine that a hammer buyer is driving a nail; her hand becomes sweaty, and the hammer slips and smashes her thumb. It might be that the sweat—or the handle's poor grip—*caused* the hammer to slip.

Now imagine that as the person hammers, she talks on a cellphone, cradling the phone between her ear and shoulder. Again she smashes her thumb. This time the causality might be the physical presence of the phone or the cognitive load of talking on the phone while performing a feat of manual dexterity. Or it could be the sweat, the grip, or more than one or all of the above.

Causality is important because it begins to form the basis of our laws, rules, norms and social convention. If working while holding a cellphone *causes* accidents, we would avoid accidents by using a hands-free kit or a Bluetooth headset. But if, say, the cognitive load is identified as the problem, *holding* a cellphone is merely *associated with* work accidents.

The hammer designer has contributed *diffused* consequences, in which he yields great power but cannot see direct causality from his actions, making it difficult to know the extent of his influence. But some examples in popular culture can help us visualize it. One person's design led to massive public outcry. When Trey Laird of Laird and Partners redesigned GAP's logo, which shows up on millions of shirts, pants, and bags, the Internet exploded with reaction, most of which was negative. Nearly 14,000 parody logos and less than four days after launching the redesign, GAP reverted to its original logo. [15] The *redesign had caused consumers to react negatively*, and the *negative reaction caused the company to lose money and brand equity*.

15 Optaros. "It's a Consumer's World. Brands Just Live in It." October 25, 2011. http://www.optaros.com/blogs/its-a-consumers-world-brands-just-live-in-it (accessed November 10, 2011).

Another person's design led to massive financial loss. Sales of Tropicana's Pure Premium juice fell by 20%, at a loss of tens of millions of dollars, after Peter Arnell of Arnell Group redesigned Tropicana's brand language. This was exactly the same juice as it was before, but the new design caused consumers to change their behavior, which in turn caused Tropicana to restore its original branding less than two months after making the change. [16]

These are design consequences, making diffused causality explicit through consumer backlash and the viral nature of social media. But design consequences also can be less obvious, with a more subtle impact on the world around us. Such consequences include our dependence on oil, the amount we pollute, our inability to attend to a task for a long period, and even the size and configuration of our houses and neighborhoods, the way we interact in groups, and the types of music or clothing we admire. A designer makes a thing, and the thing changes our lives.

Selection Consequences

Our hammer designer chose to design tools instead of restaurants, software, or systems that clean drinking water. He might like tools a lot, or his might be a well-paying job, or tools might be all he thinks to design. But his subject matter's *selection* brings consequences—still diffused, and still just as invisible and difficult to realize. So the seemingly simple decision of "which topic to focus on" will change culture's fabric and people's behavior, while dramatically advancing a value system. What if most of the U.S. industrial designers stopped focusing on consumer electronics or any other individual consumer segment? What if Apple produced flower pots instead of iPads, or the designers at Nike designed airplanes? These subject-matter decisions would have massive repercussions, known as *selection consequences*.

---

[16] Zmuda, Natalie. "Tropicana Line's Sales Plunge 20% Post-Rebranding." April 2, 2009. http://adage.com/article/news/tropicana-line-s-sales-plunge-20-post-rebranding/135735/ (accessed November 10, 2011).

A CHANGING WORKFORCE

So we find industry in a trap, stuck with designing stuff and mass-producing *consequences*. The systems and models we've structured for business—publicly traded companies, quarterly profits, company reorganizations, tiered pricing, and staffing models—prevent us from doing work that offers long-term value. But maybe this simply reflects the wants and needs of the people at these companies; are we simply playing out our collective cultural dream, to have more and more *things*?

I think it's just the opposite; my experiences tell me that many people at large companies truly want to work with wicked problems and large-scale social change, but they're systematically banned from having meaningful impact.

Students graduating with a degree in design must make the difficult career decision between a big corporation and an outside vendor ("agency," "consultancy," or "studio"). The graduates pick, often haphazardly, and enter the workforce.

When designers have been in the workforce for 12-15 months, a curious thing happens with a tremendous level of regularity, and in equal measures in corporations and consultancies. These designers come to realize that their work is meaningless. Although they enjoy the process of design, even designers at "dream companies" such as Nike or Starbucks or big-name agencies such as Accenture or Sapient find that their work doesn't fulfill them. For example, one designer described his work as "just pushing pixels around," while another spoke of a few thoughtful projects, "but for the most part, it's just making more stuff."

Although some of this discontent stems from normal level-setting that occurs after any new job, there's evidence that the problem is more generational and systemic. The students who write to me are part of the "millennial" movement (also known as Generation Y, "generation me"[17], less kindly referred to as the "entitlement generation"[18], and most spitefully as the "dumbest generation"[19])—a group that's been perhaps unfairly characterized as more demanding, more insulated, and more artificially confident in their abilities and impact. Researchers describe that this group demands more out of the workplace because we've trained them to demand more out of everything. We've told them that everyone's a winner, and we've awarded them points for effort: "60% of teachers and 69% of school counselors agree that self-esteem should be raised by 'providing more unconditional validation of students based on who they are rather than how they perform or behave.'"[20] So people of this generation probably won't be happy at any job until they find a way to have personal, meaningful impact.

---

[17] Twenge, Jean. Generation Me. Free Press, 2006.

[18] Marshall, Brigid. Current. November 6, 2008. http://www.odemagazine.com/exchange/3746/the_entitlement_generation_gone_broke (accessed November 14, 2011).

[19] Bauerlein, Mark. The Dumbest Generation: How the Digital Age Stupefies Young Americans and Jeopardizes Our Future. Tarcher, 2009.

[20] Twenge, Jean. Generation Me. Free Press, 2006.

And that impact is largely about social consciousness. Cone Communications' Millennial Cause Study identified these commonalities:

- 89% of Millennials said they are likely or very likely to switch to a brand associated with a good cause (price and quality being equal).
- 83% said they trust a company more if it is socially/environmentally responsible.
- 78% said they believe that companies have a responsibility to join them in this effort.
- 74% said they're more likely to pay attention to a company's overall messages when that company shows a deep commitment to a cause.
- 61% said they feel personally responsible for making a difference in the world. [21]

These statistics suggest the need for design to extract itself from business, and for educators and society at large to map new career or life paths for those who feel their work needs social and cultural depth and meaning.

---

21   Cone, Inc. "The 2006 Cone Millennial Cause Study." 2006.

ALEX PAPPAS
ON INSPIRATION

So many in my peer group truly want to work on positive things, to create a better world, yet the options are far too few! We have the troops, but we seem to be lacking the leaders—the people and the companies that can lead us toward attainable "good" goals. And well, if not us—the educated and enthusiastic ones who wish to help—then who?"

I had fun, learned a lot, and made a lot of money working at a company that gave me many opportunities. When I left, it felt like I was letting down the other people on the team. But I think that kind of lifestyle made me soft and made it easy to ignore the things that really matter.

I've made a conscious decision to change the things I work on and the way I spend my time.

As I reflect on my change in priorities, I'm surprised to learn how much I had begun to identify myself with my job. When you tell someone you're a toy designer, chances are you're the first one they've ever met, and they all think it's the most amazing thing in the world. And for someone who went to art school and who always doodled in class, it felt like a huge achievement to turn thinking of ideas and drawing them into a monetizable skill. I am still proud of it, but too much of that came to define me.

My job began to separate from the lifestyle I wanted and the things I believe in. Although I worked on some projects that did add value, most didn't. And it's not that company's—or any company's—fault. It's just the nature of working in industry, which is in the business of mass-producing stuff. I started to question—if we don't need a new version of that thing, why are we making one?

EXISTING APPROACHES TO SOCIAL ENTREPRENEURSHIP

Social entrepreneurs create social capital through the creation of a product, interaction, or service. They typically have backgrounds in sociology or public policy, see the world through a lens of policy or economic incentives, and develop solutions by working their way "down" from a given policy or business model. That means they'll work on either changing the policy or economics, or supplementing laws. For example, this type of social entrepreneur may start by thinking about the lack of enough low-income housing in a given city. Thoughtful solutions in this case may include offering vouchers, subsidies, or other forms of free or lower cost housing for those that qualify.

Solutions to problems viewed from a policy perspective typically take the form of nonprofit businesses or nongovernment organizations (NGOs) that work alongside government to influence change. This change may itself take one of two forms:

- one-on-one interaction with someone afflicted with a problem, as in a case manager working with a homeless person. Or,

- a lobbying effort, a top-down approach, in which someone attempts to influence policy decisions at a local or federal level.

In both cases, grants or donations typically fund the work, and many social entrepreneurs find themselves entrenched in the complexities of the legal system, government agencies, and foundations. The impact to be had in these contexts is often slow and painful. Nonprofits "abhor change," and this abhorrence creates an overly conservative approach to impact.[22] According to Nonprofit Management Consultant Nell Edgington, nonprofits typically have five problems:

1. an inability to raise enough money
2. a lack of strategic direction
3. an inability to "move the needle" on a social problem
4. a disconnected, disengaged, ineffective board of directors
5. a lack of sufficient organizational infrastructure[23]

The operational *and* strategic nature of these problems implies that these institutions often have difficulty delivering any impact at all. Because a nonprofit or an NGO constantly chases grant money and funding, they are unable to drive cultural change.

---

22 Godin, Seth. "The Problem with Non." September 15, 2009. http://sethgodin.typepad.com/seths_blog/2009/09/the-problem-with-non.html (accessed November 14, 2011).

23 Edgington, Nell. "4 Things Every Nonprofit Needs." June 15, 2011. http://www.socialvelocity.net/2011/06/4-things-every-nonprofit-needs/ (accessed November 14, 2011).

SHORT PROJECTS, SHALLOW FOCUS

The "old design"—the creation of artifacts for consumption—has traditionally been managed in the form of individual projects. This is most obvious when a consultant works with a client. The typical engagement works like this: A client—often a large corporation—identifies a problem that requires design skills. The client assigns a budget and a timeline for solving the problem. The consultant then receives the "project," which is a finite engagement with a beginning, middle, and end.

The project as a unit of engagement is so ubiquitous as to be nearly unquestioned, and because it is the common container in industry, it has become the common container in education as well. Most schools have integrated the accreditation-driven push towards assessment and learning outcomes, where formal criteria for success are established prior to learning and the student and faculty are judged against these criteria upon learning's completion.

Most design studio classes are focused on the "project," a finite course of study in which students work through the process of design to arrive at a solution to a real or simulated situation. Students conduct research, synthesis, ideation, evaluation, and reflection, and then the project is over. Typically, it's documented in a portfolio, and it allows the student to say, "I made this thing." It also becomes the core item that is assessed—somewhat objective measurements can be compared to the project outcome, and a design professor (or, more likely, an administrator) can say "85% of our students satisfactorily achieved objectives A, B, and C on the project."

Studio project-based learning is convenient. At the end of the semester, the student—and faculty—moves on to the next design problem just as a consultant moves on to the next project. The finiteness feature allows for evaluation. And project-based learning typically forces reflection-in-action, as it occurs in a studio environment with a teacher as informed guide and students supporting one another through critique, with all of the studio culture that designers reflect upon as critical for their training.

The Problems with Projects

But a project-based (and implicitly, short-term) approach to design is flawed for these reasons:

Designers fail to gain deep, tacit knowledge

Design, in any context, requires the acquisition of *tacit knowledge*—an understanding of the unstated, implicit qualities of the problem space. This knowledge often holds critical truths and assumptions about behavior, policies, norms, and values. Tacit knowledge is gained through experience, rather than through explicit instruction. It's considered to be one of the defining qualities of expertise, but because it isn't stated or written down, people are often unaware that they possess this knowledge. It may take weeks of observation to become aware of the intricacies of tacit knowledge in other people, which a short-term project-based approach to design doesn't provide.

Designers fail to gain meaningful trust and relationship with all stakeholders

In addition to understanding a given discipline, designers need to build trust with the stakeholders in a project. This trust comes through proven success—by achieving small and incremental gains with mutual and obvious benefit. Designers frequently bemoan the ignorance of project stakeholders with comments like "if only they would listen to me" or "I don't understand why they won't just do what I want"; these comments show the importance of mutual trust, which permits a designer to explore various design options.

Designers lack accountability after the project is over

The finiteness of the studio project, in academia and in professional services, abdicates responsibility to those being served. When the project is over, the designers disappear, often leaving the intended users frustrated, with a partial solution that may or may not have positive implications. This model isn't just socially irresponsible; in the educational context, it's the opposite thing we should be teaching students who want their careers to focus on social innovation. Project-based thinking reinforces the hands-off "not my fault/what can I do?" attitude that led us to the sustainability mess we've only begun to recognize. And it continues to drive a "design *for*" mentality in which designers conflate their expertise in design with expertise in a particular social problem and assume they know best.

Designers assume unrealistic expectations
Additionally, project-based learning reinforces the artificial idea that meaningful impact can occur in a short time frame—often as little as three or four weeks. Design students don't have the experience to doubt this, and when they encounter project after project that feature such time frames, they come to expect this as the norm. So they graduate without the patience for a longer engagement; they haven't learned how to stay the course.

Agencies that offer grants traditionally award them only to projects. And it does seem to make sound financial and investment sense to support these engagements with a finite time frame, a clear set of objectives, and measurable levels of impact. But that it isn't how real life works. So to attract grants, we must learn to craft a narrative that acts as though social impact is immediately measurable—as though poverty is an engineering problem.

If the "project" is a wicked problem, the solution is an extended engagement, one that allows users to become designers and designers to become empathetic. That means we need to find new frameworks for designers to operate within. This translates to entrepreneurship, where the focus is not on starting and finishing a project, but on forming a company.

The Problem with Scale
Scalability is the idea that a solution can be extended beyond a small, local group to serve a large, broad group. Typically, scale implies spread across geographic boundaries, often into new countries. And implicit in a push for scale is the idea that a solution can be generalized; the goal is often breadth of impact, but also streamlined production and distribution and a minimization of costs. The same forces that push business to scale are at play when discussing the scale of impact—the desire to

leverage sunk costs, optimize infrastructure, and crank out as many units as possible for the same price.

The field of social entrepreneurship is relatively new, and its recent surge in popularity can be attributed to this practice of scaling, where a proven intervention model is replicated in other geographic areas to spread the impact. Organizations that invest in social entrepreneurs have driven scaling efforts.

Since Ashoka was founded in 1981, the nonprofit foundation's budget has increased from $50,000 to $30M. One of its largest initiatives is its Fellows program, which offers funding and support to people who drive social change. The Fellows have tackled problems ranging from energy to microenterprise to violence and abuse. In nearly all cases, the emphasis is on civil engagement, economic development, and education. [24]

The mission of Skoll Foundation, founded in 1999 by Jeff Skoll, the first president of eBay, is similar to Ashoka's. It provides grants to social entrepreneurs in economic and social equity, environmental sustainability, health, institutional responsibility, peace and security, and tolerance and human rights. [25]

Founded by Nobel Peace Prize winner Muhammad Yunus in 1997, Grameen Foundation funds microfinance institutions in developing countries, which in turn offer loans to poor people. These loans may then be used to build agriculture infrastructure, to buy supplies, or to expand a small business. [26]

Ashoka, Skoll, and Grameen have had a demonstrable and positive impact on the developing world. Their grant recipients typically form NGOs or nonprofit companies to provide human services, education, or policy guidance

---

24 Ashoka. Ashoka - About Us. n.d. http://ashoka.org/facts. (accessed November 14, 2011).

25 Skoll Foundation. About. n.d. http://www.skollfoundation.org/about/ (accessed November 14, 2011).

26 Grameen Foundation. "Who We Are." n.d. http://www.grameenfoundation.org/who-we-are (accessed November 14, 2011).

to effect social change. These companies, at the urgency of the granting foundations, constantly focus on quantifying impact through metrics and statistics. This form of quantification helps compare investments and measure institutional performance, similar to manufacturing processes that attempt to identify and eliminate defects, and business measurements that quantify the average revenue per user. These efforts eliminate ambiguity and attempt to mechanize production to drive scale. In the case of the NGOs, "production" is the treatment of disease or the elimination of poverty, so scale of impact seems like a meaningful and important goal.

As social entrepreneurs identify a way of solving a problem—say, a new service to teach a culture about the transmission of AIDS—they attempt to codify the operations for this service and extract as much value out of it as possible. This demands scaling the solution to as many people as possible, while simultaneously reducing costs and increasing efficiencies.

The problem, though, is that scaling a solution makes it subject to a problem of mass production, or a template solution. To reap the benefits of the massive gain in efficiency requires the creation of a single, rigorous, homogenized solution. And this is precisely where large-scale social problems differ from the marketing-driven approaches that have fueled big consumer brands. Social problems are too complicated and they vary too much from place to place to benefit from templates.

A focus on scale makes a great deal of sense for social impact that's strictly commodity-driven, and make no mistake: This impact is critical. For things like malaria vaccinations, where the solution is a mass-produced artifact, the ability to optimize production and distribution is the only way to make solutions available to billions of people in need. But this approach doesn't account for the solution's inherent human qualities such as training, cultural norms, value structure, religious rules, supply-chain relationships, and power dynamics. These emotional and subjective qualities are not "nice to haves" that can be applied at the end of a project to make stakeholders feel good. In both developing countries and in the U.S., these qualities are repeatedly referenced as the "make or break" defining characteristics of adoption. Understanding and respecting these qualities build trust and respect.

Consider, then, the implications and limitations of a pursuit of scale, with respect to these subjective qualities of culture. And funding sources and the social-entrepreneur community constantly push social-entrepreneurship activities to pursue scale. For example, a system to serve the homeless in Mumbai may have a lot in common—such as providing education, vaccination, and food and water—with such a system in Rio. But the *details of implementation* need to be wildly different. The service ecology, the relationships between people, the food itself, the time of day the food is served, the way "vaccinations" are described, the relationship between men and woman, and the religious influences in the area, all must be different for the service to succeed.

A designerly approach to social entrepreneurship is one that celebrates depth of impact over breadth of scale. It is an approach that focuses on the mysterious "fuzzy front end" rather than the mechanization and mass dissemination of a solution, and one that recognizes cultural differences as being critical to success. This approach should operate alongside the great humanitarian programs described above that emphasize scale, but within the realization that metrics related to scale of impact are not sufficient for design-driven innovation.

RYAN HUBBARD ON IMPACT

I didn't like the term "wicked problems" when I first heard it. I now think it's useful to talk about. Everything is related to everything else, deeply intertwined, with so many unknown consequences. As an example, when you're trying to do economic development in a poor area—such as a city with few resources and many residents who have health problems, little education, and weirdly distributed (if any) skill sets—it's hard to know where to start. Say you start with jobs. You can try to create jobs by attracting manufacturers, but they may find too few workers with necessary skills. You could try to build that workforce by investing in job skills programs, but then the graduates don't have jobs waiting for them.

You have to pick something very concrete and very tiny, and not worry that you won't fix all aspects of the problem. You start on one of the smaller problems, someone else focuses on something else, and eventually, after a long period of seeing no change, you will have enough scaffolding—support base—in place for the community to enjoy some results.

For example, in a project to combat homelessness, people might say things like "Man, I used to sleep on the street, and it's terrible. But now I have this great base of support. I have my case manager, I talk to him on the phone, and I have a good relationship." The guy who did say it lived in transitional housing with three people who were going through similar experiences, so they would hang out and go shopping together. The project gave him skills he needed and the support he needed to function in life. We all need that. I have my family, my friends, my education, my job. All these things keep me off the streets at night. Few homeless people have them, but they need them to thrive—independently and interdependently—in society.

You can focus on one of these skills, some education, better family connection, or a case manager, but any one of those things is not enough to lift them out of their situation. Homeless people need all of those things to work before they can move off the streets. So our job is to pick one of these and make it a little better. And we hope someone else who is part of a bigger program will work on another thing. Eventually all these things fit together and give people the skills and support base to be independent and interdependent, able to exist in society as a contributing member.

Working in communities, you may find lot of people who are creative, entrepreneurial, and capable of helping their community. But you also may find they lack skills or resources to make a difference. So while you provide some direct service, you also must build the community's creative capacity. You must hire and train people from that community and bring in resources. And you need to make connections so other community members can access those resources.

Dealing with wicked problems is not just about showing up and building houses, giving things away, or delivering any direct service—even if you're in the community for the long haul. You have a moral imperative to build capacity, to enable the community to solve its own problems, lift itself up. If you're not helping the community build its ability to improve either its skills or its support network, you're not making a difference.

A DESIGNERLY APPROACH TO SOCIAL ENTREPRENEURSHIP

Designers can change culture, change behavior, and advance a system of values, and social entrepreneurship provides the economic vehicle in which designers can tackle wicked problems. For example, looking at a problem such as obesity, let's compare a scientific approach with a designerly one.

The scientific approach would use objective knowledge to produce optimal behavioral rules, with the expectation that people would follow those rules to reverse their obesity. Objectively, obesity is related to genetic dispositions, quantities of nutrients consumed, levels of physical exertion, and more. The nutrition component can be treated like an equation, with the various data of a human beings turned into an algorithm to produce the optimum diet. Exercise can be planned in a similar fashion to calculate sufficient burned calories or the ideal pulse rate. The scientific approach provides an objective "right thing to do"—eat this much of that, exercise this much. But getting people to do the right thing often proves difficult for a host of reasons, including established cultural norms, poor education, peer pressure, lack of financial and geographic access, lack of time or will power, and more. A designerly approach looks for factors that contribute to negative behavior and tries to shift them through some form of designed intervention. The constraints for the designed intervention include the cultural norms, access to education, the physical and financial access of the users, and all of the other qualities that acted as barriers to the more objective or scientific approach.

For example, looking at culture, you would find that the highest rates of obesity occur among population groups with the highest poverty rates and the fewest years of education. So a design team might spend time in these communities, observing, interviewing, and interacting with their residents. [27]

The team would look for factors beyond the nutritional qualities of food, such as *access to* fresh food: For example, the team may identify

---

[27] Drewnowski, A, and SE Specter. "Poverty and obesity: the role of energy density and energy costs." American Journal of Clinical Nutrition, 2004: 6-16.

only convenience stores in a neighborhood with few residents who have cars. Introducing a transportation program to community gardens and larger supermarkets could lead to positive behavior.

Or the team may find a culture with century-old habits that we have only recently discovered to be harmful—such as daily bacon or food cooked in fatback and lard. In this case, the strategy might include low-cost or free access to alternative cooking oils, such as olive oil, as well as education and time.

Or the team may meet people who don't know about the relationship between their health and the food they consume. An appropriate response might be free educational programs at community church or school sports events.

One quickly learns that wicked problems such as obesity demand *both* a scientific approach and a designerly approach. Because "every wicked problem is a symptom of another problem," any wicked problem is too big for a single-tiered approach. Poor people in the targeted communities don't have fresh vegetables because their neighborhoods don't have stores that sell them. That's an economic problem. They don't drive to other areas because they can't afford cars. That's also economic. They can't take the bus, because the city voted for the bus line to serve only other, less impoverished areas. That's a policy issue. The city voted that way because more voters live in more affluent areas. Now we're back to economics. And residents of more affluent areas are more likely to vote because they learned the democratic process (education), whereas poor people might have missed those lessons because of inferior schools in their districts, which again come down to economics.

A "designerly approach" embraces a methodical and often exhaustive form of craftsmanship, achieving success through informed trial and error. This approach empathizes and reflects; it has an intimate view of people's aspirations and emotions. Several vivid examples of design-led culture change illustrate the power of this approach.

The examples below of Movirtu and Studio H describe "design-led social entrepreneurship"—situations where designers (as compared to technologists or business owners) have assumed leadership roles to create positive social change.

Cultural Change in Developing Countries

Movirtu is a startup that supplies phone service to rural and poor parts of Africa; its typical users, making less than two dollars a day, can't afford a phone. They buy an access card from a street vendor and use it with a borrowed or public phone. Users of the system interact with fairly basic technology (spoken menus and standard keypads, with no touchscreens or smartphones). In developing this system, the design team sought to understand how the users consider the role of a mobile phone in their lives. Two designers spent weeks in Nairobi to do research and test and refine prototypes. One of the designers, Ashley Menger, found that, for many users, "You have no address, no phone number, no way for people to find you. Facebook and phone numbers are like an address." A phone gives "access beyond where you walk each day—to news, mPesa (a mobile-phone based money transfer service), education. There is a sense of connection with world around you, and ultimately empowerment." [28]

Menger said that design research was instrumental in gaining even simple understanding and empathy. "Among the people I've interviewed for [other] research projects, there is generally some baseline for a shared experience…. This was the first time where the gap in experience felt almost insurmountable. Could I really understand the mobile phone needs of a woman living in an African slum with two children, …no running water, sparse electricity, scant food, and in fear of thugs?" [29] Ultimately, Menger and her team were able to gain both understanding and empathy through a number of the methods described later in this book.

[28] Foster, Dave. Movirtu and frog design team up to create "telecom cloud." May 21, 2010. http://tech.ashoka.org/movirtu_frog_collaboration (accessed November 14, 2011).

[29] Menger, Ashley, interview by Jon Kolko. Personal Email (November 26, 2011).

Cultural Change by Small Businesses

Studio H is a one-year program for juniors in Bertie County, N.C., one of the poorest communities in the United States. In this county, one in three students live in poverty and 95% of public-school students qualify for free or discounted lunches. The Studio H program is a unique example of design-led social entrepreneurship in action. It combines "a more abstract, experimental, fun, and subjective learning platform" with building skills such as "the confidence to try something new, the ability to think through a problem and to frame a problem in a new way, and to accept the notion that design is inherently about a chaotic magic in which the solution is almost never as concrete as, say, an algebra equation," writes Emily Pilloton, the program's designer.[30]

While a more typical approach to educational reform might try to shift policy by changing curriculum standards or changing incentives for teachers, a design-driven approach uses research to understand a larger picture of education. Design-driven innovation reframes the problem and offers solutions that offer both utility and emotionally positive changes. Studio H tackles the "wicked problems" of education and poverty by using design skills to build confidence and personal awareness in students who typically could not have escaped their low-income environment.

[30] Pilloton, Emily, interview by Jon Kolko. Personal email (November 2, 2011).

Windsor Super Market, designed and built by students at Studio H. Photography © Brad Feinknopf 2011

2 SKILLS FOR THE SOCIAL ENTREPRENEUR

This section describes the skills designers will need in order to tackle wicked problems effectively.

BUILDING EMPATHY BY DESIGNING *WITH*

For most of the history of design, the designer has enjoyed the role of creator and a quality of authorship. A designer makes a thing, and that thing is produced in large quantities, distributing the designer's vision, ideals, and values—cultural influence—into the world. In fact these days, a design and its creator's values can be introduced into the digital world in a day or an hour. Given the power of **designer as author**, critique is usually aimed at a designed thing's characteristics: how it looks, how it provides value, how easy it is to use. Outside of small circles of design historians, few people critique the values projected by the designer. But these are worthwhile questions: Does the community that will consume the thing share the values its designer projects? Are they good values? What's a framework for assessing a design solution's values, anyway?

Participatory Design

A movement of participatory design, or "design *with* versus design *for,*" attempts to address these questions of value and ethic. Participatory design involves giving simple objects and artifacts to non-designers, and working with them to visualize a new design. Participatory design has historic precedence in conversations of unions, worker's rights, and collective control over the technological workspace. According to Pelle Ehn, one of the first proponents of what has become known as *Scandinavian participatory design,* participation in the entire design process by users of the end design is fundamental to ensuring a humane design solution. He says that by eliminating the workers from the process of designing for the workers, a nonparticipatory designer has robbed those individuals of their humanity.[31] Ehn's argument recognizes that products of design are powerful.

---

31 Ehn, Pelle. Work-Oriented Design of Computer Artifacts. Stockholm, 1988.

Liz Sanders has extended participatory design research by focusing on the actual mechanisms by which participatory design can occur. She describes how design toolkits can be used to extract creativity from non-designers. These toolkits—pieces and parts that participants can arrange to create their own rudimentary design solutions with little or no craft-based experience—are known as Generative Tools, and contain two-dimensional parts such as paper shapes and photos or three-dimensional parts such as forms with Velcroed knobs and buttons. [32]

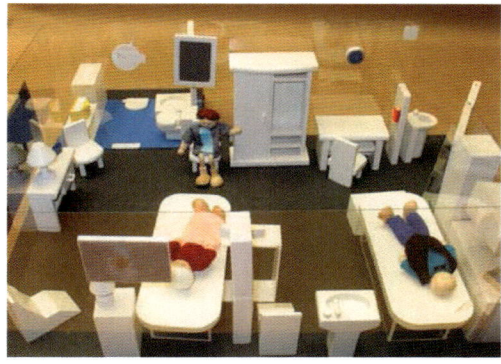

32 Sanders, Liz. "Generative Tools for CoDesigning." Collaborative Design, by Ball and Woodcock Scrivener. London: Springer-Verlag London Limited, 2000. Example image of a toolkit, used in a hospital setting, provided by Liz Sanders and used with permission.

These toolkits are given to participants who are asked to express their feelings visually about a given experience. The role of the designer shifts to facilitator—extracting creative information from "regular people"—and translator—helping to identify meaning, insight, and design inspiration in that information.

"Cultural probes" are a mechanism for directing participants' influence into the design process. The probes offer an intimate view of the emotional qualities of regular people; they do not tell the designer what to make. The designer is left to interpret these qualities and try to make sense of them. [33] These probes often take the form of artifacts that a participant completes; a common probe is a disposable camera or a journal. Designers work with the completed artifacts to reflect on or tell stories around them. Some designers will ask participants to explain the inspiration for—a given photograph, journal entry, or other creative effort. Others—such as Bill

33 Gaver, William, Andrew Boucher, and Sarah Pennington. "Cultural Probes and the Value of Uncertainty." Interactions Magazine, September/October, 2004.

Gaver—avoid asking for explanations because "we value the mysterious and elusive qualities of the uncommented returns themselves… Rather than producing lists of facts about our volunteers, the Probes encourage us to tell stories about them."

Cultural probes literally "probe" a given culture, poking at society and trying to extract inspiration through narrative. Because the input comes from non-designers, this becomes a form of "designing with," as the designer's role becomes one of interpretation and facilitation rather than visionary. This is still a fully creative endeavor on the designer's part. But consumers temper and inspire the results.

The design views presented by Ehn, Sanders and Gaver offer a comprehensive story of designing *with* rather than *for* people. Ehn promotes including end users in the entire design process, particularly when they are politically, economically or socially disenfranchised. Sanders promotes giving toolkits to end users, so they can express their aspirations and dreams without formal craft skills. And Gaver promotes probes as a way of extracting emotional and experiential insight from end users. Each technique is a theoretical framework of participatory design, as it changes the way designers think about design. But it's also a *pragmatic* framework in that it changes designers' activities and methods.

These frameworks challenge both designers and the status quo of design activities in corporations and consultancies. Designing *with* also introduces difficult questions relating to a designer's potential sphere of influence and impact. Presume that you are designing in the context of homelessness, and you have embraced a philosophy of "designing with." You seek out some homeless people to learn as much as possible about how they feel, so you can empathize with their situation.

How do you start? If you simply approach a person—homeless or otherwise—on the street and ask them how they feel, you won't get very far. Social norms dictate a different approach for engaging in conversation, and topics like *feelings* and *emotions* are usually off limits in casual conversation. To share their feelings, people need to feel comfortable speaking with you about such intimate topics, and that comfort relies on trust and respect. So to find out about the homeless, you'll need to spend a lot of time with them and *establish trust*.

Assuming you *can* establish trust, you'll probably soon encounter another social barrier: You are an outsider, so no matter how pure your intentions, you'll be viewed as part of a socio-economic (and often political) system. That is, when designers attempt to engage in social change, they are often viewed by the community they are trying to help as *part of the problem* rather than *part of the solution*.

Fundamentally, you'll need to establish an empathetic tie to the people in the community you are affecting.

The Challenge of Establishing Empathy

Empathy is a misunderstood word. Many view it as a moment in time—something finite that can be achieved as a step in a larger process. But like wisdom, empathy is difficult. To empathize with any degree of useful rigor requires a great deal of time, patience, and emotional energy.

Empathy is not the same as understanding, which is what most ethnographic tools provide. These tools help to understand context—to uncover details related to work flow or to learn vocabulary related to a particular group of people or activity. Although useful, particularly for introducing positive usability changes or adding new features and functions to a product, *understanding is not enough when designing with*. To compassionately *feel* what it is like to be another individual, one must identify with his culture, his emotions, and his style. Unlike understanding, empathy is frequently illogical and circumstantial. And this is its real value for a designer because experiences involve not only the pragmatic (activities, goals and tasks), but also the conceptual and fleeting (such as feelings, irrationality, and culture). And methods that attempt to formalize empathy can help a designer not only design for utility and for practicality, but also for emotion and behavior—the underpinnings of interaction design and the most important aspects of design in culture.

To visualize the challenge of empathy, consider a spectrum with you on one side and your next-door neighbor on the other. It would be impossible to fully empathize with your neighbor. To feel everything he feels, you would need to *actually be that person*. But you can get close. You can talk to him to understand his views on the world. You can observe his actions. You can go to work with him to see what sort of decisions he makes. With enough resources and tenacity, you could actually *become a version of him* for a short period—you could even dress in the same style of clothing, attend the same events, and hang around with the same people. But your neighbor is the unique sum of genes and experiences. His perspective of the world has been shaped over the course of his life, and that perspective affects his every thought and decision.

Empathy is formed through immersion. A designer who would foster empathetic connections with a group will spend many hours getting to know the individuals and trying to discover, without judgment, the cultural and social norms that exist within the group. Gaining the trust and respect of a group almost always requires some form of *equitable value exchange*. Unlike many formal anthropological activities, this immersion is not passive. Instead, the designer will strive to become part of the group by participating in activities, conversations, and job routines. In some cases, designers may augment their appearance to become closer to the target audience. In extreme examples, designers may actually impair or alter their bodies to better experience another person's reality. For example, Patricia Moore wanted to feel what it was like to be a seventy-year-old woman. To gain *knowledge*, Moore could have spoken with people in that group, but she was looking to build *empathy.* So for three years, she augmented her body to age it.

"I learned that putting little dabs of baby oil in my eyes would fog my vision and irritate my eyes. The look was that of eyes with cataracts… we decided to tape my fingers to simulate the lack of movement which people with arthritis must tolerate… it seemed a good idea also to restrain my movement in walking.. we put small splints of balsa wood behind each knee." Moore's technique for gaining empathy with a population was as time-consuming as it was comprehensive. And although other empathy-gaining methods are less involved than becoming another character, they all take time, patience, and immersion. [34]

Mariana Amatullo, vice president of Art Center College of Design's Designmatters program, explains that "students who do best in designing for social impact are not only skillful at problem solving but also at problem-seeking. They tend to take opportunities as moments of possibility in what Paul Light refers to as 'the Peter Pan phenomenon—that is, if you believe you can fly, you will fly.' In this sense, I find a measure of entrepreneurial intent to be essential at succeeding. With that comes the skill of perseverance, flexibility and empathy. All translate into individuals who are confident embracing constraints and operating within a context that tolerates ambiguity." [35]

34 Moore, Pat. Disguised: A True Story. 1985.

35 Amatullo, Mariana, interview by Jon Kolko. (November 16, 2011)

Students regularly attended "church under the bridge" to gain empathy with the homeless.

KAT DAVIS ON EMPATHY

When working on wicked problems, what one does can directly and powerfully affect lives. While this opportunity for impact initially drove me to work on these types of problems, I soon discovered the complicated ethical challenges of conducting research in the social space.

During my course work, I learned contextual and participatory research techniques, including the necessity of participant consent. However, as I began research on homelessness, I realized that I was not probing into someone's life habits but into someone's life. Homelessness is not caused by any one thing but by several bad decisions or unhappy circumstances, and I asked people to tell me about them. The stories people told me were so personal. Some people refused to answer my questions. Other times people opened up too much and told me things I didn't know how to respond to. Good researchers can lead a conversation toward information they want to learn about, but I often found myself just simply listening. I felt as though I constantly walked a fine line between what I was supposed to be doing as a researcher and what I felt I should do as a compassionate human being. At times, I felt more like a counselor and less like a researcher, giving out hugs instead of business cards. Other times, I simply didn't know how to respond, with my hands awkwardly in my pockets.

Many professions have codes of conduct—clear boundaries—when dealing with people in vulnerable situations. Psychiatrists never make physical contact with a patient and never talk about themselves. Social workers engage their clients only in the context of their job, not outside. While conducting research, I've wondered what those boundaries are for the designer. Are there situations where a designer should just walk away? Is it okay for a designer to make physical contact with a participant? Is there an ethical responsibility to share information with authorities if the participant talks about law-breaking activity? There must be a certain amount of trust between the designer and participant, but how far does this trust extend?

These questions are important in any design research, but even more so in the social sector, where the line between researcher and empathetic human being can easily blur.

CULTURAL SENSITIVITY

In order to shape culture, we need to understand it, and to understand it, we need to actively and continually examine it. To do this, designers go out of their way to experience trends, patterns, fashion, technology, and all other qualities that shape the communities they seek to change. What's more, this awareness requires the ability to understand and rationalize historic patterns to envision better future scenarios. This is empathy through narrative, informed by history. Narrative implies a compelling, culturally sensitive, and emotionally appropriate story that unfolds around a given user. At the most basic level, a narrative may describe the steps a person takes to achieve a goal. But its greater value is in capturing the subjective and political qualities of the society in which this goal is accomplished. Like sketching or painting, cultural sensitivity and creating a narrative are skills that are learned, critiqued, and revised over time and that require attention to detail.

Facilitating Research with Real People

Borrowing heavily from fields of sociology and anthropology, applied ethnography is a way to forge empathy. "Pure" ethnography is the study of culture through observation and fieldwork. Ethnographers immerse themselves in a culture, gather data about that culture in various ways, and write narrative descriptions of observations. Often, the output of ethnography attempts to construct a meaningful explanation for cultural behavior—positioning actions in a historic setting, and interpreting various actions and reactions.

Designers have appropriated many of the principles and techniques of ethnography, using observational research to inform design decisions. For example, Contextual Inquiry—a form of research used in information technology and human computer interaction—examines how people's work spaces, processes, and interactions can be more efficient. In corporate settings, designers commonly interview stakeholders to learn the relative desires of decision makers, usually related to features, functions, and competitive product roadmaps. And a modified form of ethnographic research is used with end users, empowering them to act creatively to visualize a desired future state of a product, system, or service.

In all cases, design-centric ethnography demands a mindset of curiosity, patience, humility, and approachability. The last two qualities are especially important because design researchers often find themselves speaking to underserved people about intimate subjects in intimate settings. But many of these participants are not used to speaking about aspirations, desires, emotions, or even the minutia of their daily lives. So ethnographers speaking with homeless people may find themselves in a sensitive position of power. Approachable and humble design researchers

A homeless man displays the items on his keychain.

can make participants feel at ease. Because they are acutely aware of how a participant is feeling, they respond to both spoken and seen cues of discomfort, anxiety, or anger.

Identifying Opportunity

Designers look for opportunities to improve the quality of life, make things easier, or change how things are done. Active design research helps to identify opportunities for designed change. But opportunities also turn up with experience in observing and interpreting trends and patterns in the man-made world. When you explore a new setting and talk to people, you'll begin to hear clues that indicate things aren't working as well as they could.

Listening Clues: Aspirations

When people describe their aspirations, they are often indicating a desired future: the way things could be, if only things they perceive to be out of their control were different. Spoken aspirations may describe long-term goals ("I just want to save enough money to get out of this hell hole") or a dream-like future state ("Someday I'll be a famous singer, too"). Behavior also indicates aspirations, although behavioral indications may be harder to interpret. For example, what's the aspiration behind a fairly obscure inner-city practice of wrapping tin foil in bicycle spokes? If you're aware of a trend towards large, expensive rims on cars, you begin to see a form of emulation, and the hidden aspiration becomes a little clearer.

Listening Clues: Discussion of How Things Used to Be

When people describe a simpler time, they are articulating desire, rich emotion, and a lot of directive data. So if you ask them exactly what about a memory produces such fond recollection, their answers typically point to areas of complexity, anxiety, or stress (often related to new technologies or cultural expectations) that can in turn identify opportunities for designed change. A statement such as "I remember when the world wasn't so complicated" should spark all sorts of follow-up discussion because it points to a pain point and a need. You can leverage this nostalgia in shaping new products and services, using feelings about the past to generate a positive future.

Listening Clues: Awareness of Negative Emotions

People are good at having and sharing opinions. You'll find valuable clues in your participants' negative opinions about things. Note that these negative opinions are typically self-directed; rather than blaming a faulty system, difficult program, or poorly designed product, people may say they "just aren't good at technology" or "aren't smart enough."

Visible Clues: Evidence of Work-Arounds

A "work-around" is a way people compensate for a technology or situation that isn't working correctly. Duct-tape, exposed wires, and missing screws are all evidence of physical work-arounds. People also engage in systemic or digital work-arounds. For example, while researching food banks, Design Researcher Ben Franck watched a woman gain admission using a photocopy of her identification that had an obviously fraudulent address manually pasted below her picture. She told him that the food bank wouldn't serve people from her real zipcode. But that turned out to be only a formality—the food bank actually served anyone in need. Her need to provide an obviously fake document indicates a system problem (Why ask for the zipcode? What's the purpose of understanding and collecting data? What is this data used for? Why needlessly embarrass your clients?) and still another opportunity for design-driven change.

Facilitating Group Creativity

Designing with literally means asking members of the community to help you design. That means inviting groups together to explain the problems, even by making things. But group dynamics bring their own problems. When non-designers need to draw, sketch, or build something in public, many become anxious or self-conscious. They consider themselves "not creative," so they shy away from producing something that will be judged. So a facilitator must encourage participants to put aside their fear of failure. This encouragement comes from an open, supportive, and comforting environment and the right words, including self-deprecating humor. It also demands a great deal of patience, an acute awareness of the needs and concerns of individual participants, energy, and passion—the same skills required for talking to potential customers in an at-risk setting. When a facilitator shows passion about the subject matter and the creative process, participants quickly tap into it as a source of energy and inspiration. For your participants to trust you and your process or methods, they need to believe you truly care about the subject matter and about them. To help them believe in you, use two powerful tools: Nonverbal Communication and Framing.

Nonverbal Communication

As you speak, you communicate nonverbally with your face, vocal tone, and body, including your posture, gestures, and movements. Make sure these mechanisms support your intended message and content. For example, maintain…

- an alert stance to convey energy and passion. (A slumped or sitting posture, on the other hand, may convey only apathy or fatigue.)
- a smile to help relax and persuade your participants, especially those who are overwhelmed by the concepts you present. Smiling makes you look relaxed, confident, and approachable.
- inclusive eye contact to engage the participants and encourage them to participate.

Framing

Before any facilitated session, research the participants' expectations, skills, and abilities. Then use the findings to make appropriate assumptions about their familiarity with the subject matter and confidence in working with groups.

Use your research and assumptions to "frame" the session in a way that presents value to the participants and explicitly defines its purpose. The frame creates the conditions that will encourage your audience to respond positively to you. It rationalizes the value of creative engagement in general and of your methods and processes in particular. The frame also sets the session's rules.

Begin each session by articulating your purpose. Then frequently remind participants of that purpose with words such as, "the one thing we are here for today is…." This will help them remain focused.

INFORMED INFERENCES THROUGH SYNTHESIS

In the context of designing for impact, one of the hardest things to know is "what is right." What is the right thing to do first? What is the right service to build? Synthesis is the leap from empathy-driven research to a new opportunity. It helps to identify what new tool, idea, system, or object might help a given user in a particular situation. Because this thinking is inference-based, *you may be wrong*. So rather than spending a great deal of time building a cohesive, final, mass-produced solution, quickly test your idea early on by pairing your inference with a rapid form of prototyping.

Synthesis is a way to apply inferences within the confines of a design problem. [36] The various constraints of the problem begin to act as logical premises, then the designer's work, life experiences, and logical leaps based on inconclusive or incomplete data begin to shape the inference.

Inference is how designers can move from problem-seeking to problem solving. Performing this inference will require malleable factual or emotional and cultural data.

Typically, action comes from verbal debate; people discuss what should happen, and a good argument will define what to do next. This "good argument" relies on rhetorical methods of persuasion that celebrate deductive reasoning and inductive logic. In both cases, historic precedent drives the argument. Deductive reasoning presents an argument based on what all have historically *agreed* to be true, while inductive logic grounds an argument in what historically *seems* to be true. When designing for impact, designers learn to trust informed intuition or inference enough to create a new thing based on a vision of the future rather than an argument from the past. This skill is learned by trying, failing, and reflecting; it starts with a deep understanding of data-driven design, and then a realization of what "just enough" means in the context of synthesizing disconnected ideas. Inference through synthesis is learned through continual and rigorous practice.

---

36 Coyne, Richard. Logic Models of Design. Pitman, 1988.

Synthesis is a process of connecting ideas, identifying patterns, building on anomalies, and otherwise making sense of a large and complicated set of data. The process happens naturally through learning; each time we read a book or listen to a speaker, we make sense of it by synthesizing the new material with our existing world-view and knowledge. But synthesis can occur artificially, too, and designers can learn to force synthesis to occur more rapidly than it might in a normal situation.

Forced synthesis typically demands a form of externalization of data: The designer acknowledges the limitations of working memory and uses a whiteboard or note cards to present large data sets. Force synthesis typically also leverages the ability to look at things in new ways. So designers who synthesize data can consider new perspectives of time (What if this event occurred over a longer period? What if it occurred instantly?) or system (What if we zoomed in to focus on that particular person or organization? How far out can we zoom and still understand?). Sketchbooks and large drawing sheets also encourage forced synthesis. That's because they both force the designer to abstract situations and ideas into representational forms. At the root of both simple tools, as in research, is curiosity to understand the human-made world. Design synthesizers constantly seek to learn how things are connected, to understand patterns and anomalies, and to view the world in new ways.

A large part of synthesis is considering and credibly explaining behavior. For example, a designer investigating health and wellness may notice that some health-club members tend to "stand around" rather than exercising or using the equipment. If asked to explain what they were (or were not) doing, the answers wouldn't be very rich, because few people are aware of their behavior at any given time. But the designer can synthesize this observation with other data, trends, and patterns to provide a credible guess to explain the behavior. Being only a guess, it can be (and likely is) wrong, but because it's used to provoke design insight, its validity doesn't actually matter. The insights are statements of provocation—guidelines, but not rules for a design solution.

Recognizing Value

Learn to create self-sufficient revenue models, and to think about finance and value alongside your creative design. Your company will need to create enough profit through its product or service offerings to pay for operational costs (including competitive salaries). That's preferable to the traditional model of impact, in which organizations doing humanitarian work rely on grant money or donations. Those organizations describe the constant rat race of chasing donations, with as much as 50% of their time, effort and resources directed at it. This distracts from the organization's core mission. But although you'll want to consider profitability, note that profitability does not necessarily mean *massive profits*, a turn-off for many in the social sector. [37]

Learning to think in terms of operational self-sufficiency requires thinking of a design's economic value and considering the world from this *perspective of value*. Value is the *worth* of a product, system or service, and worth is dynamic—it changes based on what the market, broadly, determines and what a person, individually, will pay. A loaf of bread is worth a certain amount of money in a given market on a given day, but to someone starving, it may be worth a lot more. Yet people often have trouble applying that idea to design. Even designers who realize that a product has the potential to change someone's life rarely quantify what that change may be *worth* to someone. So they fail to understand the *value* of what they've created. But you can gain an understanding of value through awareness and practice: Consider how much goods and services cost, and try to identify the motivation that led to its price. What value do the sellers assume, and how did they arrive at it?

Financial Acumen

Be skeptical of adoption, and realize that the adoption of your new products and services takes time. Expecting a massive overnight success is not realistic. A social entrepreneur must work within existing models of profit, loss and revenue for a simple reason: Nearly all other constituents

---

37 Indeed, a social business as defined by Nobel Peace Prize winner Muhammad Yunus is one that is non-loss, non-dividend: The company strives to make only enough money to reinvest in the people and the operations of the company.

will be playing by these financial rules. Social entrepreneurs also must understand the role money plays in for-profit and nonprofit companies, how various financial models work, and why they are adopted by various organizations. That does not mean that finances must be social entrepreneurs' major goal. But to ignore money is to ignore reality; designers should understand basic accounting and bookkeeping.

Many nonprofits attempt to fund themselves with grants and donations, which provides a level of resources to continue operations. But as these organizations succeed and try new programs and methods, they will feel pressure from their granting agencies to better measure their impact, to improve performance and reach, and to better and more rigorously account for their money. They'll lack control over their own destiny, as the threat of financial stability is constantly looming. And focus and attention will be redirected from their important work, and aimed at writing more grant proposals.

Some companies use a subsidy model, where the revenue produced by selling something to one group is used to offset the cost of providing a free service to another group. This model introduces complexities around fairness (how do you qualify for the free service?) but provides a service to those who may not have the money to pay for it.

Other financial models:

- "freemium": A limited version of a product is offered for free, with various features or capabilities are provided for a fee.

- subscription: A recurring fee is charged per month.

- per-usage: Each use generates a charge.

- tiered pricing: Various features and limitations are added or removed based on the amount paid.

RUBY KU
ON MONEY

Research at a homeless shelter inspired the idea for our company, HourSchool. We didn't want to become reliant on grant cycles and the fundraising model of the nonprofit world, so our challenge became finding other markets that would find value in our solutions and pay for them. The typical goal of a business is to maximize profit. But when trying to build a social enterprise whose goal is to maximize social impact, we face the challenge of balancing mission and profit. If paying customers keeps a company alive, the social impact work has a chance to address its mission. At the same time, as we grow and scale our companies, we have to be cautious about mission drift, when our work no longer addresses the needs of the original target market.

Creating social impact through ventures requires a sustained focus in an area of passion and sticking with your ideas through rounds of success, failure, and evolution. Learning to be this type of leader is less about checking off a laundry list of skills to acquire and more about embracing the entrepreneurial attitude of doing whatever is required of you on any given day. Social entrepreneurs do not let their own limited resources keep them from pursuing their visions. They are skilled at doing more with less and attracting resources from others. Ideas are powerful but will remain only good ideas until they're also proficiently executed. Well-executed companies start to create powerful impact.

PUBLIC MAKING

Learning by Making

Talking a situation into existence is what happens during most corporate meetings. But once the meeting is over, the discussion thread disappears. Participants are left with various views of the conversation, and fallible memory and attention often create a large disconnect between what actually happened and what was perceived to have happened. In fact, it's often as if the conversation never happened at all; meetings are commonly held to rehash decisions that were thought to have already been made.

We designers offer a solution for this flawed form of sensemaking, as we capture, understand, and critique our ideas by continually building artifacts—externalizations—of them. These artifacts act as a stake in the ground, a declaration of an idea ready for sharing or critiquing. In some contexts, the artifact also acts as evidence because it provides a concrete representation of decisions, discussions, and other communal activities.

This externalization of ideas can be thought of as prototyping. Situations, organizations and environments are *sketched* into existence, creating a collaborative environment for further iteration and design. The prototype acts as a working representation of an idea. As the idea changes, so does the prototype. Prototypes can include diagrams, sketches, or more finished visualizations. For example, industrial designers and architects, who deal with space and form, may build foam models of hairdryers to study how a user holds the device, or foamcore models of a physical space to achieve the best placement for various rooms or objects. Graphic designers create prototypes of brochures, pamphlets, and posters for trial, critique, and a better understanding of the experiential qualities of the artifact. But you also can build prototypes for non-physical things, such as services or interactions. These prototypes may require more planning and consideration than a physical prototype, but it's worth it. They offer designers the ability to experience things over time and react to these experiences in further iterations. There are three easy ways to spark this form of public making: sketching, role play, and storytelling.

Sketching, Publicly

One of a designer's most important skills is the ability to visualize what does not yet exist. This visualization—commonly called daydreaming—is usually done within the confines of ones thoughts. When the daydream is over, the vision is gone. A memory may remain, but without a tangible, discussable, *actionable* artifact, the future state disappears. Sketching is one way to capture this envisioned future state and communicate it to other people. Sketching serves several purposes:

- Sketching is fast. A good sketch can be produced almost as quickly as someone can describe an idea.
- A sketch can be easily changed. As an idea grows, a sketch can grow with it; ideas can be crossed out and sketched again; as an idea becomes more detailed, so too can the sketch.
- A sketch provides a log, so it can be referenced at any time. This log can be used to remember, to provide clarity, or to settle disagreements. For those involved, this log is a dynamic reference to a conversation. Each mark on the page is literally a bookmark to a point in time, and by "walking through the sketch," one can often recall decision rationales and alternative points of view.

Less obvious benefits of public sketching:

- Sketching commands respect. A sketch becomes a powerful political tool for advancing an agenda. A sketch can be vivid and quickly understandable. And because of the rarity of sketching in our culture, sketches stand out from written reports or presentations.

- Sketching holds attention. As a sketch comes to life, those watching become engrossed in the process of making. They tend to feel more connected with the subject matter and the narrative of creation.
- The sketcher becomes the center of power. The person holding the pen can choose what to sketch, how to envision it, what priority to give it, and the way it connects to other elements. In politically challenging situations, the power of this role lasts long after the sketch is finished because the sketch remains.

You'll gain the confidence you need to sketch in a public setting (on a whiteboard or a large sheet of paper) through practice and continual critique and refinement. Start practicing by considering how to sketch any conversation you have as it happens. Carry a sketchbook with you to practice describing things visually and in front of (and in cooperation with) other people.

Sketching People, with Designer Ahmed Riaz

One of the most valuable sketch subjects is people. Putting the human at the center of a design helps you and decision-makers to empathize with people. A sketch can be in any medium as long as it is a) not precious (the designer has no quams with throwing it away), b) quick, and c) useful. It can be on paper (such as the notebooks of Leonardo da Vinci or Jim Henson) or video (with YouTube or Vimeo) or in software (with tools such as Flash or processing prototypes), form (with foam or combined found objects), or even electronics (with a tool such as Arduino). A sketch is not meant to stand alone; it often needs a person to interpret it. That's because a sketch is often purposely vague in some areas so it can be more articulate in other areas.

 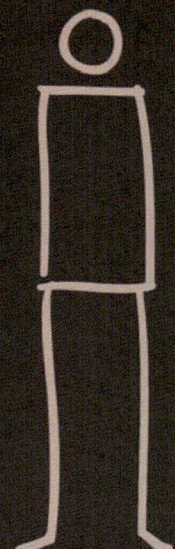 

Step 1: Draw the body as a rectangle. The torso is the largest part of the body, and the type of rectangle you draw will represent the character of the whole figure. For example, you can draw a flighty rectangle to show movement, a flirty rectangle to demonstrate a light touch, or a sinister rectangle to show anger.

Step 2: Draw an oval for the head. The shape of the oval begins to give emotional weight to the figure.

Step 3: Ground the figure with legs and feet. Think of the legs as wires coming from the two bottom corners of the rectangle. You can bend the wires into various shapes to suggest the figure's movement.

Step 4: Draw the arms. Also think of them as wires. Draw mitten hands, which are most important for describing what the figure is feeling or doing.

Role Play

Sometimes called method acting, role play is another public approach to design because it happens with (and often in front of) other people. A group acts out a particular situation, taking on the roles of those involved and using these roles to filter actions and responses. The method requires the actors to take on enough of the personality of their representative users that they can respond quickly and authentically. For many designers, role play isn't a conscious activity that's easily methodized; designers often don't even know they are doing it. Consider this example of two designers working through details of a text-based donation system:

> Jeremiah: I think it's going to be a little awkward, considering that most panhandling happens at intersections.
>
> Anne: Well, if I'm driving and you are on the corner [she pretends to move an invisible steering wheel]… if I see your sign, and it has your number on it [Jeremiah immediately holds up an invisible sign]…
>
> Jeremiah: Hi! Could you spare some change?
>
> Anne: Sure, here you go [motions to hand him some change].
>
> Jeremiah: No, no—text it to me, here, see? [points at sign].
>
> Anne, breaking character: Yeah, that's weird because it eliminates the human interaction. I wanted to just give you money because that's what I'm used to.
>
> Jeremiah: Right, and you probably wouldn't even read my sign because it's usually just Sharpie on a piece of cardboard. What if I had a completely different kind of sign or something to hand to you?

In this example, the designers seamlessly enter into a character, and then quickly extract themselves from the situation so they can understand and judge it. In just a few seconds, they identified social barriers to a design idea, and Jeremiah started thinking of alternatives. Because Jeremiah and Anne had an existing relationship with one another, neither one had to explain what was going on. Instead, they simply started acting, a form of prototyping a situation in real time, to work through the details of a human-to-human interaction.

Telling Stories

A compelling narrative creates a vision that creates a trajectory for action. It demands a cohesive storyline or plot, actors doing credible and (when appropriate) incredible things, and the ability to introduce technological advancement only when necessary.

Part of telling an impromptu story is the ability to quickly envision an alternative future, and arrive at that future in a way that's engaging. A "design idea" is not a design—it's simply the initial spark or seed of a larger narrative. It's important to bring the design idea to life by relating it to people, situations, and emotions. Consider these examples:

> It would be great if we had a mobile-phone app that allowed…

> …consumers to scan their produce in the grocery store and identify where it came from.

> …voters to scan a candidate's name in the voting booth and learn about their position on particular issues.

> …vehicle owners at a repair shop to scan a repair estimate and find out how much the same repair would cost at other shops.

All three examples are "design ideas," but none of the examples are complete narratives. How would consumers, voters, or vehicle owners know about the applications? How would they remember to use the application in any of the contexts? How would they overcome the social stigma of using an application in a community setting? How would the fruit, voting booth, or estimate be recognized—would it have a QR (quick response) code? How would the QR code get there? What's the incentive for the service provider? Would it work only on expensive smartphones? Who would update the content? Who would pay for it?

Answering such questions begins to *round out the story*—these questions, and their answers, make the narrative *credible*. Good storytellers learn to anticipate areas of incredibility, so they introduce enough detail to counter them. This doesn't mean they know the answer to every one of these details but that they offer enough of an answer that an audience can fill in the details themselves.

Being Proactive

An entrepreneurial approach is largely about attitude, and it requires *doing things* without necessarily having all of the information or much confidence in a given course of action. Many students may see a desired end state and even the steps needed to arrive at that state, but they may lack the discipline, focus, and sustained energy to arrive at their vision, and most important, to even *start*. Because of the quantity of things they have to do, they may find starting to be intimidating, which allows a natural state of entropy and procrastination to creep in.

Instead, foster proactivity by constantly articulating tactical steps: Make to-do lists, prioritize activities, do "just enough" for the time being, and focus on one thing at a time. All of this comes more easily to people who work in companies where meetings and run ins with colleagues in the halls prompt activity. In other environments, proactivity may require faking or forcing these prompts to action by setting artificial deadlines or establishing external meetings.

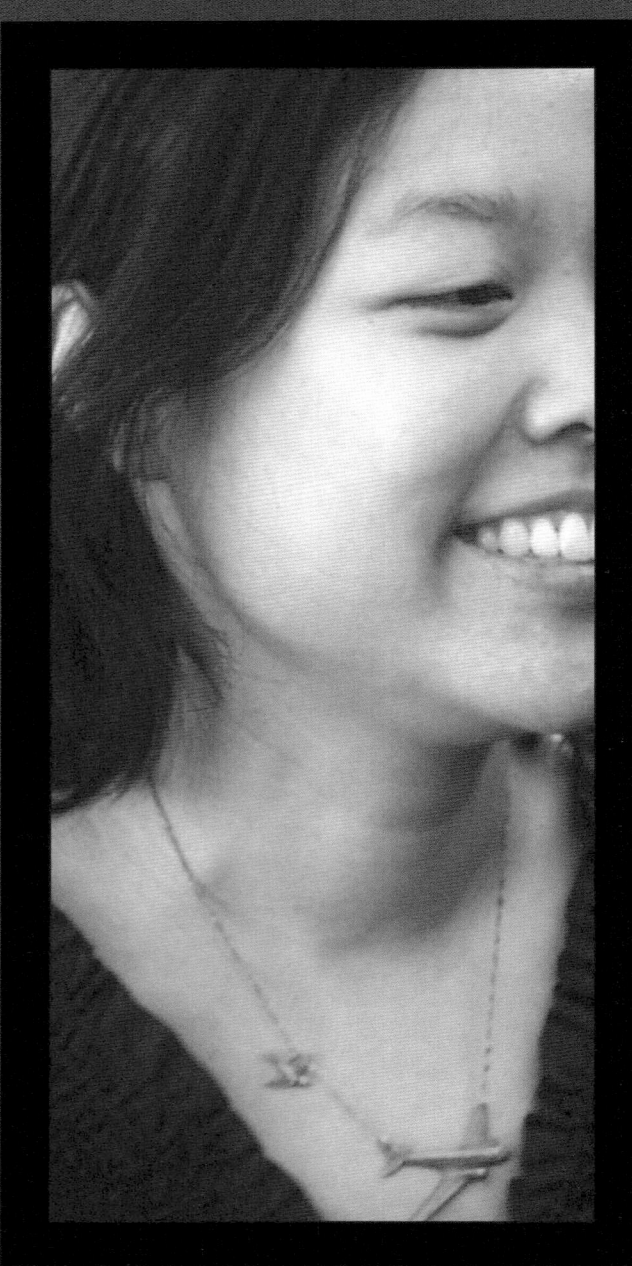

CHRISTINA TRAN
ON MOMENTUM AND FOCUS

Research is no excuse to delay designing. Design is no excuse to stop researching.

After procrastinating for weeks, waiting for interviews that kept getting rescheduled, we plunged in and started designing. And we kept talking to people. We were doing many steps in the design process simultaneously: research, synthesis, design, and development.

Each time we did anything—conduct an interview, move forward with our coded prototype, or draft our story—it felt as though we could get deeper and more specific. It reconfirmed for me the value of rapid prototyping—even if it's often difficult to just start. The design process is messy, individual, and unique to the needs of each project and project team. I'm starting to embrace that messiness and have to keep reminding myself that there is no right answer to where we should be in the process. The only wrong answer is to do nothing.

These continued research/synthesis/prototype cycles are likely to happen naturally if you focus during a given time on one specific social issue that you feel passionate about. So the next piece of advice I would give any designer who seeks to apply their creative skills toward activism and community engagement, and social impact is to commit to a place, to live and work there, and to apply your skills to that community's benefit. You will continue to learn more, talk to more people, and have experiences within the relevant field; and the insights you'll gain from following your curiosity will continue to inform your design work.

This idea of deep engagement makes me question the consultancy model of design in which you come into an issue, work for a predefined amount of time, and then leave. It's what rubs me the wrong way about the recent surge in design "competitions" that call for submissions from creative citizens to solve problems that are remote to people's lives—physically and emotionally. If I want to tackle maternal health in Africa, I may be able to contribute my ideas from Austin, but I lack 1) context, 2) skin in the game, and 3) responsibility for what happens to those ideas. It feels more productive to me either to engage a curated group of people (including designers) who have committed to the issue or to co-design with the African mothers.

With social issues, where our solutions will have real positive and negative impact, commitment to the process and its consequences is important. We designers must be willing to throw ourselves into an issue space for an extended period and to partner with real experts and actual stakeholders. Especially while I'm in my 20s when I don't want to plan beyond next week, commitment to anything is difficult. But if I want my work to have social impact, and I do, I think it is a step I must take.

3 TEACHING AND LEARNING

This section describes a model for teaching and learning social entrepreneurship. If you're an educator, the model will help you change an existing curriculum. If you're a practitioner, it will help you structure your own course of study without enrolling in a formal program.

COMMON MODELS OF DESIGN EDUCATION

Like any other broad career path, Social Entrepreneurship can be taught and learned. Adopting such a curriculum in educational institutions requires changes that may be threatening to those who are invested in existing models for teaching design: Bauhaus, Integrated Product Development, and Design Thinking.

The Bauhaus Model

Nearly every design school in the United States and Europe begins with foundational studies, including two- and three-dimensional design, typography, color, composition and more. These typically studio-based courses follow the Bauhaus model, focused on craft, formgiving, and problems of aesthetics, functionality, and usability. Students learn by doing, and the "doing" is often long, arduous, and methodical.

For example, students may learn color theory by assembling and comparing collages of different colors or by painting large canvases with a single hue or by mixing their own paints to duplicate a series of color swatches. In a subsequent class, students may learn three-dimensional design principles by creating sculptures.

As a result of this education, students learn how to create artifacts—printed posters, physical products, brand elements, pamphlets, postcards and signage. This work involves a number of core competencies, including color theory, two-dimensional design, three-dimensional design, typography, composition, printing and prepress, packaging, digital prepress, logo and mark creation, and more. Perhaps the most important contribution of the Bauhaus model has been an appreciation of craft and an understanding of how to teach and encourage it to create a level of substance and value.

For example, at Rhode Island School of Design—one of the best-known design schools in the country—freshman take classes called Drawing Studio, Design Studio, and Spatial Dynamics Studio. [38]

---

38 RISD. Foundation Studies. n.d. http://www.risd.edu/Academics/Foundation_Studies/ (accessed November 14, 2011).

Savannah College of Art and Design—one of the country's largest art and design schools—offers freshman classes called Drawing I: Form and Space; Design II: 3-D Form in Space; and Design III: Time. [39]

The Integrated Product Development Model

This model, which emerged in the late 1990s, was developed, in some respects, as a rejection of the Bauhaus model and a response to business needs; hiring managers found graduates' skills insufficient to participate in product development. Integrated Product Development (IPD) brings together marketing students, students of design, and students studying engineering to focus on a comprehensive plan (including marketing rollout and product features and changes). The small, integrated quality of the team allows for agility in decision-making, and the combined skills help to ensure that the resulting product meets market and user needs, and that it can be produced in scale. As a result of this education, students are prepared to work with or as brand managers in large companies, bringing products to market quickly and effectively. For example, at Carnegie Mellon University, future Masters of Product Development graduates take a capstone course that is actually called Integrated Product Development, which emphasizes "identifying, understanding, conceptualizing and realizing new product opportunities. Through the course, interdisciplinary student teams partner with industry sponsors to bring these new opportunities to life. Some even result in patent applications." [40]

Perhaps two of the most valuable lessons that emerge from integrated product development are the idea of collaboration within interdisciplinary teams and the role of facilitation. Designers, marketers, and engineers solve problems in strikingly similar ways. But the subtle differences are critical. These differences emerge only after a long period of working together, as teams begin

---

39 SCAD. Foundation Studies. n.d. http://www.scad.edu/foundation-studies/courses.cfm#programButtons (accessed November 14, 2011).

40 Carnegie Mellon University. Integrated Product Development (IPD) course. n.d. http://www.cmu.edu/mpd/capstone-course/index.html (accessed November 14, 2011).

to realize words like *specification* and *design* and *value* have different meanings depending on perspective. Facilitation extracts meaning from all participants, even when the participants may not agree on process, method, or outcome.

The Design Thinking Model

As a progressive model with roots in design education, design thinking has found its way into business school as a way of driving innovative decision-making in organizational change. MBA candidates learn to look at situations in new way by empathy building and divergent thinking. This education helps students engage in a broader level of institutional discourse; in addition to marketing or advertising a product, they also can focus on strategic planning related to the entire trajectory of the business or organization.

One of the most valuable qualities of the design-thinking model of education is inference-based action with a focus on moving quickly to prototyping. The model encourages students to move through a tangible form—often a diagram or a three-dimensional model—to create something, try it, discuss it, and learn from it. That tangible form can provide leverage in politically charged corporate debates about organizational change. For example, at Stanford's "d.school", students take a course called Design Thinking Bootcamp, where they study "design processes, innovation methodologies, need finding, human factors, visualization, rapid prototyping, team dynamics, storytelling, and project leadership." [41]

The Problem—and Opportunity—with All Three Models

All three models firmly embed design in the context of artifacts intended for humans. Yet although they have offered tremendous value to students and educators, the models continue to advance the message that design is inextricably linked to consumption and that the only place a designer can build a career is in the world of business. But, as this book illustrates, design can be equally embedded in public policy, in education, and in the social sector. In fact, design may better fit these

---

41   Stanford. Design Thinking Bootcamp: Experiences in Innovation and Design. n.d. http://dschool.stanford.edu/classes/#design-thinking-bootcamp-experiences-in-innovation-and-design (accessed November 14, 2011).

other areas given its suitability for solving problems related to the human condition. Design "aimed" in any direction will bring valuable results. If we aim it at footwear, we'll realize innovations in shoes. If we aim it instead at problems of poverty or inequality, we'll realize innovative solutions to those problems. Yet most design students are taught to aim it only at the Fortune 500, so they graduate with a desire to practice in the context of money and mass production. They may ultimately tackle wicked problems, but there is huge potential for curricula that explicitly emphasizes such work. *This* is the opportunity for design educators: to teach a design model that leverages the benefits of Bauhaus, Integrated Product Development, and Design Thinking models—while helping students realize they can position design in any context.

A CURRICULUM TEMPLATE

The following social-entrepreneurship and design curriculum can be taught to—and applied by—students with little or no background in design (or engineering, marketing, or any other "making" discipline) in the context of large-scale social problem solving. The program is a work-in-progress and is not **the** model of design education for the future. But it is **one** model of design education for the future, it has experience-derived features, and qualitative evidence supports it as a strong pedagogical approach for other institutions to build upon. These other institutions need not be limited to colleges and universities; the curriculum's materials can help to prepare grade-school students for literacy and fluency in a changing world. Nor must the institutions be "academic"; a corporation or consultancy can teach the materials internally or use them to help clients understand the process of designing for impact.

The curriculum departs from the three traditional educational models described above in a number of key ways. Students engage in traditional graduate programs to gain skills, knowledge, inspiration, and contacts. In addition to these common goals, this curriculum teaches students how to start a company with a "double bottom line": focused on both operational self-sufficiency and social impact. Students identify an opportunity for impact, develop systems and products that drive value, produce working prototypes, learn the basics of company operations (including budgeting, sales and marketing, and branding), and focus on creating an entity that is financially self-sufficient, so they can pay themselves the salary they want while they do the work they want to do.

The program explicitly pairs classes in methods ("how to" classes) with theory classes to encourage constant reflection related to the nature of social change. Students learn to understand systemic consequences and to act with a sense of purpose and responsibility in their design decisions. Although both are critical in any design program, they're of utmost importance in a design program focused on changing behavior: Students graduate with both a massive amount of power and a sense of humility about how to wield it.

This program provokes debate and reflection by presenting alternative, conflicting, and often-extreme viewpoints through readings and an influx of guest speakers. Students are forced to develop a Theory of Change related to their core business and to constantly challenge and evolve this theory.

Formal Outcomes and Assessment Tools
Like other curricula, this program measures success through a set of outcome statements which describe skills students should have acquired by the time they complete this curriculum. Students self-assess their progress towards these outcomes four times during the academic year and then get back their self-ratings when they graduate. And every week students film video-reflections on entrepreneurship and their academic study.

Demonstrate a comprehensive process for solving complicated, multi-faceted problems of design.
Our students learn a process of design that can be applied to any type of problem. In demonstrating their competency, students need to be proactive and to understand what action to take at what point in the process. This is learned through experience; students begin by following a process in a rote manner, but they slowly learn to customize the process for their unique design problem.

Develop original design approaches to large-scale social problems.
Students learn to direct their design efforts towards problems that have a meaningful impact on society. This implies design judgment—students learn to articulate a value structure and judge design problems within the structure's context.

Develop a unique vocabulary of criticism as related to technology, allowing objective and comprehensive responses and critiques to large-scale design problems.
Our emphasis on mindfulness requires our students to learn to examine design opportunities and solutions from a critical perspective. And this requires students to understand the unique context in which a design opportunity exists, build relationships and empathy with stakeholders, and offer a thoughtful opinion on the existing and desired state.

Demonstrate the creation, application, and verification of new forms of design research that improve on the state-of-the-art.

While our students learn existing and leading design research methods, they quickly begin to see shortcomings in these methods as applied to social and humanitarian research. As a result, students must craft their own research methods and successfully apply them with users and other constituents.

Develop and document new models to present various types of qualitative data.

As students gather large amounts of research data, they are challenged to present this material in ways that clearly describe the research and help the audience form an educated opinion of the material. This results in a highly visual model of the data and its interpretation.

Develop original synthesis forms that re-contextualize familiar thought patterns.

Fostering innovation and extracting insights demand assigning meaning to the gathered data. Students learn to create their own synthesis forms—often large-scale documents, maps, charts, and diagrams—to extract the most value from research activities.

Develop original methods of framing issues, resolving conflict, and parsing complex situations into actionable objectives.

Conflict generated during design is often productive and critical for advancing the quality of a given idea. Students learn methods for engaging in productive design criticism and conflict; they are expected to create their own frameworks for judging ideas and resolve contradictions within the context of a design activity.

Cultivate a culture of speed in the creation of demonstration prototypes to stimulate the collaborative process.

Students learn to quickly represent their intent and to communicate their designs to stakeholders and to receive criticism on the ideas. Fundamental to this outcome is the idea of designing publicly; students are constantly pushed to work confidently with and around other people in a studio environment.

Create interactive working prototypes of digital design problems that allow for comprehensive user testing and the communication of diverse and complicated ideas.

Students are expected to constantly evaluate their design solutions by gathering data from end users. During the project's pilot phase, students must present a working prototype of their solution, system, or service for comprehensive user testing. In many cases, students are urged to pilot test a simple and small piece of a larger solution.

Compose scholarly documents of publishable quality that explore the nature of design and rigorously defend the assertions used to construct the argument.

It's critical that students be able to intellectually reflect on the impact of their design work; scholarly contributions allow students to participate in the larger discourse related to designing for impact as they allow other designers to build upon the knowledge created during the design process.

Participate in the global design infrastructure that exists within the business and academic world.

Professional conferences, publications, and other engagements give design students the opportunity to reflect on their own situation, process, and methods—and compare their learnings and accomplishments with those of their peers and industry mentors.

Invent new forms of behavioral prototyping that inform the designer at an early stage in the design process.

Designing complex systems and services requires unique forms of prototyping. Students need to be able to envision a future, and produce a low-fidelity representation of that future. This may include acting through scenarios and creating digital or physical artifacts,.

Develop the vocabulary to discuss design solutions with other members of a product development team.

Students learn to clearly articulate their design ideas to team members of other disciplines.

Develop the vocabulary to defend the social value of their design solutions.

Students learn to speak the language of value, as pertaining to the social and humanitarian benefits of a solution, and to appropriately frame their solution in the contexts of the problem space and the people they are serving.

Student Christina Tran works through a process of provocation and ideation.

Curriculum Structure

The curriculum balances traditional lecture-style knowledge transfer with the creative learning-by-doing, experiential style of the design studio environment. Students rapidly gain knowledge of various humanitarian issues along with advanced design knowledge of synthesis, service and system design, and entrepreneurship. Much of the curriculum is focused on a 32-week thorough investigation into one humanitarian issue. This period permits the students to propose, prototype, analyze, and evaluate multiple iterative design solutions. As students progress through the curriculum, they work collaboratively in a studio environment that supports rapid ideation, informed trial and error, and an immersive process focused on ethnographic user-centered design research and synthesis. Courses are run formally—with syllabi, assignment/project briefs, and ongoing critiques and evaluations—yet studio projects maintain an "incubator" feel, focused on the production of functioning solutions.

The curriculum presents three types of classes—methods, theory, and the application of these methods and theory in a studio environment.

The curriculum is structured to challenge three false assumptions of students typically bring to a new academic program:

First, most students have a dramatically incorrect view of how much work they can accomplish in a certain amount of time. The curriculum appears overwhelming until they learn to work more quickly, efficiently, effectively, and confidently.

Students also bring the assumption that there is a right answer to their work and that the teacher knows it. This curriculum constantly challenges students to find the right course of action or the next step on their own. They are left to apply learned methods as they see fit.

And students typically view work as a finite process; they expect to "end the work" at some point. This curriculum challenges that perception because students leave the program when they have just begun their own companies and social initiatives. But it's important that students feel a sense of closure upon graduation, so this closure needs to be introduced artificially through presentations of milestones; students cannot be led to believe they will "solve" a problem like poverty in 32 weeks.

TEMPLATE CURRICULUM
COURSE SEQUENCING

	Quarter 1	Quarter 2	Quarter 3	Quarter 4
Methods	Interaction Design Research and Synthesis	Rapid Ideation and Creative Problem Solving	Evaluation of Design Solutions	Entrepreneurial Practice
Theory	Interaction Design, Society and the Public	Service Design	Theory of Interaction Design & Social Entrepreneurship	(None)
Application	Studio: Foundations	Studio: Research & Synthesis	Studio: Ideation and Development	Studio: Pilot

ENTREPRENEURIAL DEVELOPMENT

Research	Synthesis	Sketching	Building	Pilot
Domain Research User Research Market Research	Synthesis Themes Opportunities Topic Narrowing Detail Research Theory of Change	Wireframing Service Blueprinting Feature Identification Business Model	Prototyping Testing	Testing Iteration

MAJOR EMOTIONAL MILESTONES

- Students have accumulated topic-specific knowledge and emotional substance
- Students have identified a single Big Idea to pursue, and have begun to visualize it
- Students have identified and visualized a core set of features and created a service blueprint
- Students have developed a working version of their Big Idea and have arranged for a group of people to test it with

Launch
Further Incubation
Further Iteration

Students have completed a pilot study and have formulated an entrepreneurial plan for their core business

TEMPLATE CURRICULUM
INTERACTION DESIGN RESEARCH & SYNTHESIS

Course Description

This course focuses on methods of qualitative design research and design synthesis used to approach complicated problems of technology, behavior, and society. Students learn techniques and processes that allow them to gather data in the field, analyze that data in a rigorous and substantial way, and extract multi-dimensional insights, meaning, and trends.

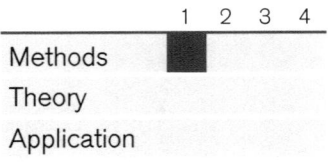

Course Outcomes

As a result of taking this class, students will:

- be able to apply methods of qualitative design research, including contextual inquiry and participatory design, to a large-scale interaction design problem

- be able to apply methods of design synthesis, data mapping, work-flow, task-flow, and concept modeling to a large-scale interaction design problem

- understand the role of research and synthesis in the design process

Course Content

Students learn how to leverage their curiosity and rigorously conduct ethnography. Working in teams, students develop a research focus related to a large and ambiguous topic (such as "food" or "poverty"). They learn to structure a formal interview guide that helps plan and organize an interview, and to conduct the interview; they then juxtapose this with a more informal, fluid, work- and events-based contextual inquiry. In class, showing videos of the activities, the professor leads group critique, pointing out both opportunities for redirection or further probing, and potential obstacles, such as where the interviewer asked leading questions or overstepped a cultural boundary.

Students create written transcriptions of their work and contextual design work models that describe the flow of information, the use of artifacts, the various power structures in place, and the sequence of actions. These too are critiqued in a group setting to identify areas of vague interpretation, unnecessarily large jumps in meaning, or areas that weren't modeled at a sufficient level of fidelity.

Finally, students learn to conduct participatory design sessions using rudimentary toolkits and other visual artifacts. They create ways to extract creativity and meaning from nondesigners. Again, the process and results are critiqued.

TEMPLATE CURRICULUM
RAPID IDEATION AND CREATIVE PROBLEM SOLVING

Course Description

This course teaches methods of creative problem solving and ideation, including sketching, drawing, diagramming, and the underlying approaches of abductive and divergent thinking. Students learn how to quickly visualize ideas, iterating through variations to allow ideas to evolve effectively.

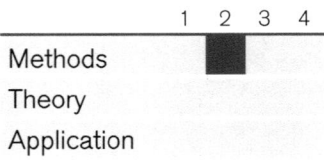

Course Outcomes

As a result of taking this class, students will:

- quickly visualize ideas through various tools, including analog and digital sketching, rapid physical prototyping, whiteboarding, and diagramming

- use diagrams to model complicated systems and services, provoke facilitation, and design discussion and rationalization

- communicate through sketching, both formally and in a real-time facilitation

Course Content

Students learn how to think in narratives and visualize artifacts in the context of story. Emphasis is placed on the development of digital artifacts such as software or apps because of the low cost of producing them and the ease of introducing them into most cultures. Specifically, students learn how to write narratives and differentiate between problem states and future states. They set goals and articulate future states in which users can better achieve their utilitarian and aspirational goals.

Students then learn to visualize complex systems through the use of concept maps and other diagrams. They must hand-sketch these diagrams, to habitualize graphic facilitation as a thinking skill. The diagrams are used to facilitate discussion between professor and student and between stakeholders in various project settings; students learn to change and augment their thinking on the fly and on the spot, by literally changing the diagrams with a marker.

Finally, students learn how to create wireframes—schematic representations of digital systems that show how users work with the digital tools to achieve goals. Students learn how to ideate quickly, moving from a hand sketch to a crisp and refined visualization; ultimately, they learn how to produce interactive simulations they can use to articulate how a given tool works and how it can function or provide value.

TEMPLATE CURRICULUM
EVALUATION OF DESIGN SOLUTIONS

Course Description
This course teaches methods of evaluation and testing that thoroughly analyze a design in an attempt to refine it. Students also learn forms for documenting design changes. And they learn to propose design suggestions that are technically feasible and appropriate for a given target audience.

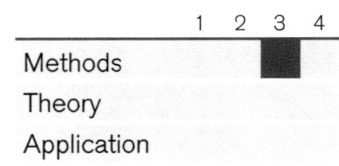

Course Outcomes
As a result of taking this class, students will:

- plan an appropriate testing session to gauge the usability, usefulness, and desirability of a particular interaction design

- successfully conduct various forms of qualitative and quantitative user testing and understand the tradeoffs among them

- document and describe evaluative findings related to comprehension, appropriate implementation, and desirability

- judge and manage contradicting usability and desirability data, and apply this data to the iterative design of a given product, system, or service

Course Content
Students learn to use and assess a series of evaluation methods, including:

1. Think-Aloud User Testing. Using this method as a primary tool students learn how users solve problems and think of the systems and the tools they encounter.

2. Heuristic Evaluation. Students learn to compare their creative design solutions with existing guidelines and best practices. They also learn when to best argue for differences between their point of view and commonly accepted guidelines.

3. Cognitive Walkthrough. Students examine their designs from the perspective of a new user, and they evaluate the learnability and immediate accessibility of their creations.

4. Surveys. Students study the complexity of conducting a survey properly, gain an understanding of rigorous sampling by evaluating multiple examples of flawed survey design, and learn survey vocabulary.

The course focuses on the rapid and continual use of think-aloud testing during product and software development, so students practice testing interfaces at various levels of fidelity and finish.

TEMPLATE CURRICULUM
ENTREPRENEURIAL PRACTICE

Course Description
This course describes the financial models and structures of business, as related to launching a particular design product, service, or system. It introduces students to organizational structures, for-profit and nonprofit business activities, and product introduction and distribution methods.

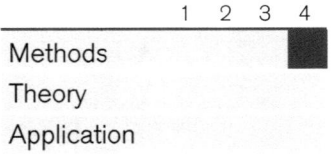

Course Outcomes
As a result of taking this class, students will:

- be able to write a cohesive plan for introducing a given design solution, including describing the design's value, the business plan, the timeline, and dependencies related to the solution, and plans for growth and continued refinement

- understand the methods of legal organizational structure that enable a successfully implemented design solution

- be able to appropriately describe the entrance (and, if necessary, exit) strategy for a given design solution

- be able to address—in both writing and in personal interactions—concerns of potential investors, donors, and other interested parties

Course Content
This course introduces students to the business fundamentals, vocabulary, and tools needed to establish their own company and consider the more pragmatic, less creative aspects of running it. Students learn to create a financial model for revenue, profit, and loss, and to plan appropriately for adoption rates of their products and services. Students create pragmatic documents intended to support the organization of their business, including articles of incorporation, contracts, policies, and procedures. Students also go through the process of creating a legal entity, while learning about the various organizational models that make sense for profitable, impact-driven organizations.

TEMPLATE CURRICULUM
INTERACTION DESIGN, SOCIETY, AND THE PUBLIC

Course Description

This course emphasizes the theoretical, social, and political relationships between design and social culture. Students learn theory and discourse related to designing for the public sector, specifically as related to ill-defined problem solving and the ethical obligations of designers.

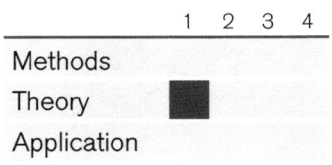

Course Outcomes

As a result of taking this class, students will:

- be able to articulately discuss and debate issues of interaction design for social impact

- be able to cite scholars and designers who have framed interaction design problems in social impact

- demonstrate a point of view that describes the role of design and design thinking in the context of social impact

Course Content

Students explore readings by various thought leaders with various perspectives. Conversation in class is largely based on directed questioning by a professor, and it involves constant comparisons between authors. Students learn to compare arguments (both in substance and approach) and to form an opinion on the larger discussion topics.

At the end of each section, students work in pairs to produce a position paper—a short document that argues for a given point of view, requiring a synthesis of multiple readings. Students realize the complexities of collaboration and the need for artifacts to capture systems and broad viewpoints. They use their learned modeling techniques to produce visual representations of their position papers.

TEMPLATE CURRICULUM
SERVICE DESIGN

Course Description

This course introduces the advanced design topic of service design, with a focus on the service design blueprint.

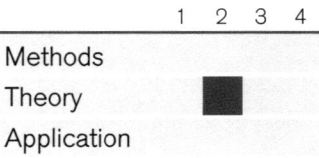

Course Outcomes

As a result of taking this class, students will:

- understand the unique elements of service design

- use ethnographic research to collect service and customer data

- use customer journey mapping to frame a design problem

- be able to create a service design blueprint

Course Content

Students learn to understand the relationship between people, products, policies—and the services that contain them. Emphasis is placed on understanding the rhythm and placement of service touchpoints (places of engagement with a user), and the relationships among them. As students examine existing services, they learn to create maps—service design blueprints—to visualize how a user might experience the people, products, rules, and behaviors of the service. Students indicate breakdowns in communication, utility, or value, they identify ways to improve the service, and they use the blueprint as a guide for product-development activities and launch.

Ultimately, students develop an understanding of the relationship between users and other people in a service. They learn that design includes the organizational theories, rules, and policies that dictate human-to-human interaction. Emphasis is placed on service ecology: a way of thinking about services that emphasizes freedom, exploration, and a more "hands-off" approach within a contained series of boundaries. This theoretical approach to design shifts from "building artifacts" to "building scaffolding."

TEMPLATE CURRICULUM
THEORY OF DESIGN & SOCIAL ENTREPRENEURSHIP

Course Description

This course teaches interaction design theory as it relates to dialogue, discourse, semantics, experience, and communication. Students will explore the philosophical and sociological aspects of technology in the context of wicked problems in society and culture.

	1	2	3	4
Methods				
Theory			■	
Application				

Course Outcomes

As a result of taking this class, students will:

- be able to describe complicated issues of design theory as related to design practice, and understand the role theory plays in actual design

- understand the historical underpinnings of the methods and processes used in design

- understand how to ground design decisions in a historical, philosophical context

Course Content

Students explore academic discourse and literature related to interaction design history, mobility, creativity, strategy, experience, and innovation. They explore readings from a diversity of perspectives and learn to present artifacts synthesizing divergent viewpoints into a cogent and cohesive argument.

Students explore the relationships among interaction design history, the progression of technology, and the introduction of mobile computing into developed and developing countries. Next, they examine the relationship between creativity and management, investigating the role of design strategy in shaping how organizations approach difficult problems. Finally, students read about poverty, developing countries, and social innovation, synthesizing the readings into a larger framework for considering the technological world.

TEMPLATE CURRICULUM
STUDIO: FOUNDATIONS

Course Description

This studio course teaches the fundamental methods and processes needed to conceptualize, communicate, and sell ideas in today's complex environment. Students are exposed to various social media and prototyping tools and techniques.

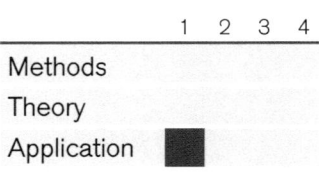

Course Outcomes

As a result of taking this class, students will:

- be able to create and maintain a social presence that builds their brands online

- be able to maintain a blog that captures their course work, grows their brand thesis, and engages the community at large

- be able to effectively communicate ideas both visually and verbally

- be able to build digital prototypes that illustrate their ideas

- be able to select the appropriate prototyping tool and medium for any given problem

- be able to build their understanding of business innovation cycles

Course Content

The course introduces students to design, emphasizing the role of *making* in *communicating*. Through a series of activities, students develop a personal brand statement and produce designs that provide value to users and substantiate the brand offering. Students learn to think publicly, using blogs and other communication mechanisms to build a following. They identify how to quickly and effectively produce things that can be refined and judged. They develop an entire design solution to bring an idea to life, and they learn to test the desirability of the solution with end users. Students also learn to treat their work as imperfect and transient; at the end of the quarter, they abandon their solution to reflect on their learning and apply their process in subsequent quarters.

TEMPLATE CURRICULUM
STUDIO: RESEARCH AND SYNTHESIS

Course Description

This course continues the Interaction Design and Social Entrepreneurship deep dive. Students will conduct research and synthesize data relating to that research, in the context of a humanitarian and social problem space. Students will gather data through qualitative methods of contextual research, analyze that data, and begin to identify trends, patterns, insights and opportunities for design.

	1	2	3	4
Methods				
Theory				
Application		■		

Course Outcomes

As a result of taking this class, students will identify:

- patterns and trends in the context of a real, large social problem

- opportunities for interaction design solutions that can positively affect human behavior on a large, social scale

- design constraints and parameters within which to build design solutions

Course Content

Based on an extremely large topic statement ("Food" or "Poverty"), students engage in research with an at-risk target population. Students write a research plan that describes their intended methods, research time, population, and script. Students then use the appropriate research methods to learn about the social problem and user wants, needs, and desires. Research methods may include contextual inquiry, interviews, cultural probes, participatory design activities, and immersion. Students systematically manage research findings through transcriptions and large walls covered in research data, and they continually refine their research plan to reflect that learning.

Students synthesize their research, methodically extracting insights and articulating patterns and anomalies. They combine these materials into structured design themes, and they work through a process of massive conceptual ideation, identifying hundreds of potential design ideas. Students rule out ideas based on an evolving theory of selection. They ultimately produce a small set of storyboards that describe an opportunity, define a potential intervention, and begin to hint at a design idea for change.

TEMPLATE CURRICULUM
STUDIO: IDEATION & DEVELOPMENT

Course Description
This course is the next phase of the Interaction Design and Social Entrepreneurship work. Students will begin to prototype and test designs related to a given humanitarian and social problem. They will build physical and digital artifacts as needed to describe their design solution and will test those artifacts in the actual context of the design problem.

	1	2	3	4
Methods				
Theory				
Application			■	

Course Outcomes
As a result of taking this class, students will:

- illustrate, through prototypes, sketches, and presentation materials, a cohesive design idea to positively address a particular large-scale social and humanitarian problem

- describe and rationalize the design decisions that have led to the development of a particular design solution

Course Content
Students develop detailed design artifacts and working prototypes of their products, systems, and services. If they are producing a piece of software, they will create a wireframe for each screen and an interactive simulation or prototype of every key aspect of the tool. If they are producing services, they will create service blueprints and necessary artifacts to rollout and test the service. These artifacts may include printed materials, scripts, or policy definitions.

Through iterative critique and usability testing, students quickly refine these design artifacts to increase their value and usability. A large portion of the course time is spent considering and revising detailed design decisions—specific labels, wording, interactions, artifacts, instructions, or other nuances.

TEMPLATE CURRICULUM
STUDIO: PILOT

Course Description
This course is the last phase of the Interaction Design and Social Entrepreneurship work—students conclude their design efforts, producing a high-quality prototype of their product, system, or service. Then they conduct a pilot launch with real users, so they can judge the design's usefulness. They produce appropriate contextual information to present their work, then present it in an open forum.

	1	2	3	4
Methods				
Theory				
Application				■

Course Outcomes
As a result of taking this class, students will:

- be able to describe a complete design solution for a particular humanitarian and social problem or opportunity

- illustrate a comprehensive understanding of interaction design in the context of social entrepreneurship

- understand how to design for society and culture, and how to clearly articulate that understanding

Course Content
To understand the value of their design work, students launch a pilot of their business, using a prototype to work with real users and gauge the usefulness and usability of their work. The prototype frequently is incomplete in that it offers only partial functionality or requires more-than-desirable manual processes. But students learn the value of their work with their target population. They also begin to better understand stakeholder opinions and values, areas for improvement, and ways to improve the product, system, and service.

Most of the course is spent conducting the pilot. This includes training, assistance, observation, and in-context usability evaluation. Only a small part of the course is devoted to securing the pilot population, which may involve working with NGOs or nonprofits to gain access to users. Students often have secured relationships with these organizations through previous research.

Finally, students describe the value of their work, articulate a plan for further revisions, and retrospectively articulate the positive and negative qualities of their process and methods.

4 METHODS

This section contains methods—stand-alone techniques—that you can use as you take on wicked problems from an entrepreneurial perspective. Some of the methods are for conducting research and gaining empathy, while others are for making sense of data and coming up with new ideas. There are also methods for building financial models and worksheets to help you target financial success.

METHODS FOR CONDUCTING RESEARCH AND GAINING EMPATHY
CONTEXTUAL INQUIRY

What is it?

Contextual Inquiry is an ethnographic research method that helps to understand what people do and why they do it. The method was created as a way of capturing work's complexities: information flow, the cultural qualities of a working environment, and the sequence of routine tasks. Contextual Inquiry relies on three main principles: focus, context, and partnership. Researchers establish a *focus* for the information they want to learn and as a filter for subsequent actions and activities. The focus helps identify the *context:* the specific environment to be studied. This may be an office, a home, or even a place as specific as an airplane or a coffee shop. The focus also directs selection of participants for research, and it is with these participants that the researchers will try to form a *partnership*. This partnership is characterized by qualities of apprenticeship—the researcher is an apprentice, hoping to learn as much as possible from the master. This education occurs by watching real work and by probing with questions.

How do I do it?

1. Identify a focus. What do you hope to learn? A focus may be broad, as in "We are seeking to understand how people save money." Or it may be specific, as in "We are seeking to understand how people manage their credit cards each month and what relationship families have with budgets and financial limits." Derive your focus from the various constraints of the work; relate it to the human opportunities that you will explore.

2. Use your newly identified focus to determine the context you seek to understand. The context might be a physical environment—literally, a specific business or place. Or it might be a digital or theoretical environment—a website, an online community, or a community or group. To make subsequent steps easier, define the context with as much detail as possible.

3. Identify the participants you seek to work with— the various stakeholders, constituents, workers, managers, or consumers who make up the given context. Again, provide as much detail as possible.

4. Reach out to the potential participants and schedule a time to observe them. Unlike traditional research forms that extract the participant from the context of the work or activities, in contextual inquiry, you watch real activities in their normal context, and use these activities to provoke questions and answers. When you attempt to schedule meetings, make clear to potential participants that you intend to observe work. This will be a strange idea to them, and so you'll need to explain how watching work helps you more than simply asking and answering questions. Gaining access to the context is often the hardest part of the entire contextual inquiry process.

As you begin to conduct the contextual inquiry, consider these basic guidelines:

- Suspend judgment. As you attempt to form a partnership with your participants, consider how you can prove to them that you truly want to learn. This means that when you discover inefficiencies, problems, or strange behavior, simply note them for later interpretation rather than calling attention to them, attempting to correct them, or implying that they are wrong

- Be curious. To learn, you need to ask questions, and probe for details. When your participant mentions "he", find out who "he" is. If the participant uses an artifact, ask about it. Try to extract as much information from the participant as possible by asking as many open ended questions as you can.

- Have a plan, but be ready to deviate from it. For example, plan enough questions to fill the amount of time you've scheduled even though

METHODS FOR CONDUCTING RESEARCH AND GAINING EMPATHY
CONTEXTUAL INQUIRY, CONTINUED

you may decide not to ask them; ideally your observations of the participant working will inspire new questions on the spot.

- Treat the participants with respect. Remember that you are literally and figuratively intruding on someone's life, so be courteous, supportive, forgiving, and empathetic.

When should I use it?

Contextual Inquiry is a broad method you can apply in a number of contexts. It can act as the centerpiece method for your research and understanding. For example, you can conduct a contextual inquiry when you want to learn how people do things—how they complete their work, how they spend their time off, how they purchase things, or how they manage their finances. You might conduct it at the beginning of product development to help you understand users' needs and desires. But contextual inquiry also identifies the vocabulary people use to describe things, so you can also use it throughout the development of products, systems, or services to ensure that users understand your design intent. And you can use it to identify how people think about a given problem, or when you sense an opportunity for design-led intervention but are unsure about the or details.

What is the output, and how can I use it?

Contextual inquiry begets data—a great deal of it. The entire contextual inquiry is often recorded, using an audio or a video recorder or both, and the recordings transcribed. You can then create models as a more vivid, visual representation of the transcription. These models may emphasize workflow, influences, and power dynamics or the artifacts, services, and systems that support work.

Learn More
Read *Contextual Design* by Hugh Beyer and Karen Holtzblatt, the method's developers. ISBN 1558604111

POCKET HOTLINE

Created by Chap Ambrose & Scott Magee

While we were students at Austin Center for Design, we noticed an overwhelmed front-desk attendant at the local homeless shelter. With a line of homeless people out the door and the phone ringing off the hook, the attendant could not help clients in a meaningful way but was left to give just enough information to move along the visitors and callers. At the same time, we realized that many people want to help the homeless, but most of them don't know how, so they may volunteer only during the holiday season. We saw an opportunity to leverage the volunteers to ease the information-distribution bottlenecks.

We developed Pocket Hotline to connect people who seek a sympathetic shoulder. We used cheap or free mobile technology to tap into a large group of motivated volunteers. As the platform developed from an outsourced call center of volunteers, we realized the same model could apply to other nonprofit and even to for-profit endeavors whose customers need accurate, timely information.

Commercial clients pay monthly subscriptions that subsidize some of the same service for nonprofits and other social enterprises. This subsidy model worked to address one of the main challenges we faced as new social entrepreneurs: Creating value does not equate to profit. Social impact is now part of the equation where the betterment of human lives is an achievable outcome. Profit helps us run a business, but our focus and goal is on developing social currency—making the world a better and more equitable place to live.

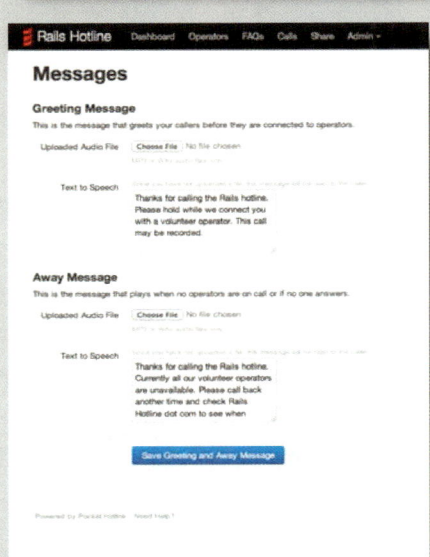

METHODS FOR CONDUCTING RESEARCH AND GAINING EMPATHY
PARTICIPATORY DESIGN

What is it?

Participatory Design is a broad label for creative activities that are done *with end users*—where designers act as facilitators or visual translators for people who may not be skilled or confident in idea expression. The activities can take many forms, but the most common ones use visual and semantic tools—such as stickers, blocks of words, or ambiguous shapes—to offer expression to nondesigners. Participants are prompted to use these tools to create their own interfaces, products, services or systems. After creating these artifacts, participants answer the designer's questions about what they've made, to identify their creative intent. Participants also may begin to articulate their feelings about specific visual or semantic qualities.

How do I do it?

First, recruit your participants. Target those who represent your target audience—people who will actually use your service, system, or product once it's created. Schedule 60- to 90-minute meetings for the actual session, and encourage participation by meeting with two or three people at a time. Be sure you have a dedicated place for them to work, but consider that the place can be where your participants feel comfortable (their homes or businesses), rather than where you feel comfortable.

Next, create a toolkit of visual stimuli, such as shapes, pictures, or symbols; they don't have to relate to the design context. Assemble 50 to 100 visuals, with each printed on its own piece of paper. Visuals often are iconic forms such as phones, coffee makers, automobiles, or chairs. They also include characters expressing emotions, such as happiness, sadness, frustration, and confusion. The visuals may also include images of environments, such as parks or offices; shapes, such as circles, squares, or triangles; textures, such as grittiness; or materials, such as rubber or metal.

Also assemble parts, related to the form and material of your design direction. For example, if you are designing software for an iPhone, you would gather iPhone interface elements, such as buttons, inputs, and other controls. If you are designing a physical tool, assemble handles, grips, and other physical elements that might be appropriate for the tool design. Choose pieces and parts that are appropriate to the intended platform or medium. If the design team is open to a broad range of media, include a variety of parts.

During your participatory design session, ask the participants to use your toolkit materials to visualize their ideas; then provoke them with specific requests related to your topic. For example, if you are trying to understand the relationship between lower-income households and food purchasing, you might ask the participants to pick images that best represent their feelings about food, food preparation, food purchasing, or eating. Or you might ask them to create their ideal kitchen, using kitchen parts (appliances, cabinets, counter-tops) and raw materials.

As participants build their ideas, try not to disrupt them, but do encourage them if they become shy. Many people will need verbal affirmation to get started, and you might work alongside them so they can see how to go about the exercise. You might need to ask them questions as they work, like "Why are you adding that?" or "What does that shape represent to you?"

Once they've completed an exercise, ask them to explain their design to you. Ask open-ended questions to understand the various details created and choices made. Be curious, but objective, avoiding evaluative statements, such as "That's excellent!" or "That would never work."

When should I use it?
Run a participatory design session when you want to better understand how people think about a given problem, discipline, technology, or aspect of culture. The method can give clear insight into their vocabulary, their priorities, and the things they value. The method can be particularly useful in contexts that are hard to observe, such as things that are private, culturally sensitive, infrequent, or expensive. And because the creation of ideas can be less threatening than an interview about practices, the method can also be useful in situations that are politically charged or that have a particularly obvious power relationship at play. For example, if you are working with the victims of domestic abuse, creating a model of an ideal living space can be more fruitful than conducting an interview about the pros and cons of shared living space.

What is the output, and how can I use it?
Participatory design may result in video, photographs, transcriptions, and artifacts. The method doesn't dictate what to build, so you can expect the resulting artifacts to be low-fidelity, messy, and incomplete. But the output of these sessions can provide valuable insight into priorities and can motivate strategic design decisions and directional alignment. You can position this output in various stakeholder-facing media to argue for a particular direction.

Learn More
Read Liz Sanders' papers on her website, www.maketools.com/papers.html

METHODS FOR CONDUCTING RESEARCH AND GAINING EMPATHY
CULTURAL PROBES

What is it?

A cultural probe is a documentation device, such as a workbook, worksheet, disposable camera, or tape recorder, that is given to a participant with instructions on how to complete it. For example, the participant may be instructed to answer the questions or do the activities on one workbook page each day at lunchtime, or to take photos of various situations or circumstances. The participant completes the artifact on his or her own and returns it to the designer, who analyzes and interprets the results.

Designers of cultural probes often craft a narrative to further integrate the probe into the life of the end user. For example, instead of just asking users to tape-record things they want or desire, a designer may embed the recorder in a pillow, call it a "dream catcher," and ask users to record their dreams each morning when they wake up.

How do I do it?

Identify the type of people who will use your probe; they should match the target audience of your product, system, or service. Then list the types of data you want to gather from the audience. For example, you may want to know the audience members' daily activities, their long-term aspirations and dreams, or their feelings about certain people, situations, or products. In listing your desired data types, make your list as specific as possible; "aspirations related to long-term financial behaviors, such as saving, investing, and purchasing" is more actionable than the vague "financial aspirations."

Then think about the best situational context in which a participant should describe the data you want. So, for data related to finances, think about a participant's typical physical location when they consider personal finances. What time of day would it be? What would they have with them? Who would be around them? These associated qualities begin to describe an opportunity for a probing interaction.

A cultural probe, designed by Ashley Menger.

106 Wicked Problems

Next, sketch the probe as you think about specific activities or questions related to the situation. If you're interested in aspirations related to credit card debt and financial planning, you might sketch a worksheet for users to fill out each time they pay a bill. Or you could create a series of short questions, placed on users' credit cards, for users to answer each time they charge something. The probe-development process is typically iterative. Your probe must include instructions. Although you'll discuss instructions with your participants, they are likely to forget how to use the probe, so it should stand on its own.

When the probe is ready, test it with someone you know without interpretation or evaluation. Present the probe as you intend to with the actual participant, and be sure to write instructions. When the tester completes the probe, ask the person to highlight confusing tasks and suggest further improvement before the probe goes to real users.

Refine the probe, recruit users, distribute the materials, and remind your users to complete them. As part of the research plan, you might call or text users each evening or at another planned interval. If your probe use extends beyond a week, schedule an in-person meeting or review with the users at a mid point.

Finally, collect the probes and interpret the results. Pay special attention to things that surprise you, anomalies within a given user's data, words participants use to describe things, and situations, images, or emotions that stand out. Extract insights from the data and include these insights in your war-room or insight wall.

When should I use it?

Use the cultural probes method to explore emotions, aspirations, desires, and other fuzzy human qualities. Because the probes are completed without your physical presence, you'll receive provocative and evocative data that will probably inform the more qualitative aspects of your design solutions.

What is the output, and how can I use it?

Depending on the type of probe, the output may take the form of written comments, spoken words, pictures, or drawings. Cultural probes produce unedited "raw" and often rich data, and because it is literally created by the users, it tends to act as a strong voice during further design and development efforts.

Learn More
Read "Cultural Probes and the Value of Uncertainty," an article by Bill Gaver. It's available online.

METHODS FOR SYNTHESIZING DATA AND DEVELOPING IDEAS
2X2

What is it?

A 2x2 is an organizational diagram used to illustrate how many things compare across two dimensions. Within a single dataset, a 2x2 can show trends, outliers, and areas of saturation and scarcity. In the context of design, this diagram can describe opportunities for impact and areas ripe for innovation. It also can be used to determine the relative quality of design ideas. Because the 2x2 maps one criterion on the x axis and an alternative criterion on the y axis, the grid of four quadrants show all possible combinations of those two criteria.

How do I do it?

Decide which evaluation criteria are most important for your particular context, and label the axes with this criteria. For example, if you are synthesizing raw data from your research, you might map "urgency of problem" against "prevalence of problem"; this mapping would describe how common you think the problem is, and how critical it is to solve it quickly. If you are synthesizing initial design ideas to understand which to pursue, you might map "feasibility of solution" against "potential impact."

Next, draw the 2x2 in big scale. A large wall is ideal, with painter's tape for the axes.

Make a card for each data point you are evaluating. For example, to evaluate utterances from a contextual inquiry, you would write one sentence or utterance per card; to evaluate design ideas, you would draw idea per card.[42] In a group of participants—including designers and other stakeholders—read each card aloud, and make sure everyone understands it. Then, plot each point on the graph. When you find the proper place for each point, stick it to the wall with tape or a pushpin.

When you have about ten data points on the grid, revisit the first few. You may need to reposition them because you placed them before you had a point of reference. As you progress through the data, continue to re-negotiate space; especially when you have data points stacked on top of each other, reposition them as needed.

When you have mapped all of the data, examine the results. Look for a story you can tell about the data concentration in the center of the map and in each quadrant, particularly the extreme corner areas. Why is that data interesting? What commonalities appear? How can you describe the path from one corner to another?

---

[42] Generate cards quickly by exporting an Excel spreadsheet to mailing labels (using Microsoft Word's "mail merge" feature).

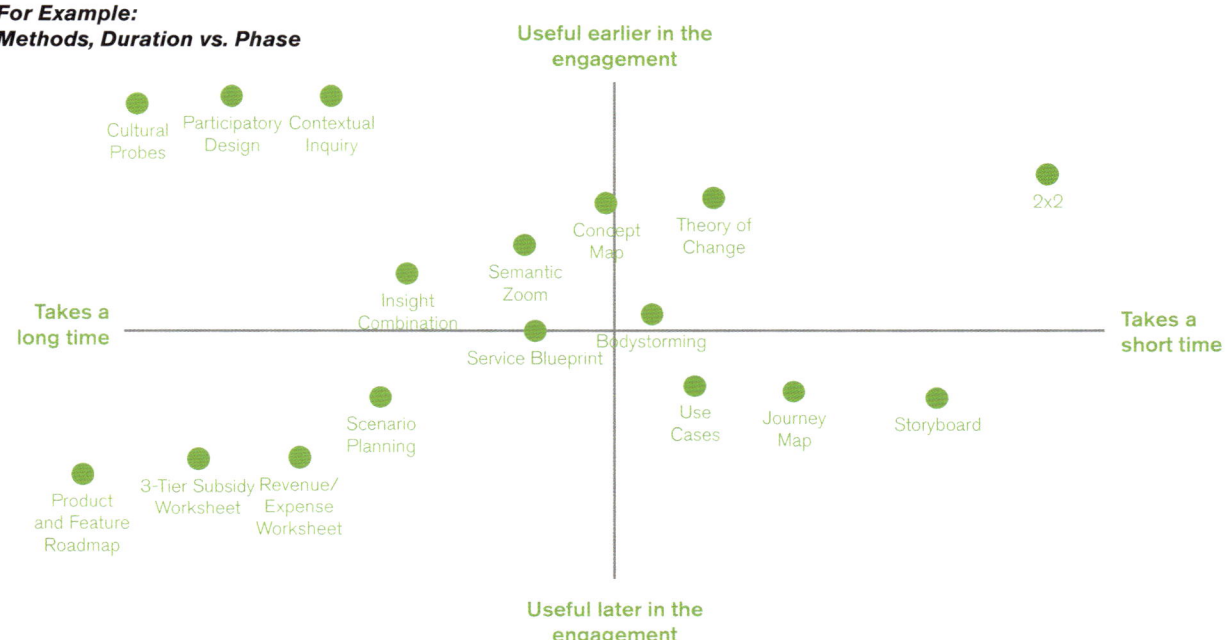

When should I use it?

Use a 2x2 when you have a large data set that you need to make more manageable or memorable. You might make a 2x2 on the first day of research and continually revise it over the course of your investigation. Or you might make one during ideation and design—as you produce ideas, you can map them to understand their relative appropriateness.

What is the output, and how can I use it?

The 2x2 itself acts as a tangible artifact you can present to stakeholders; in fact, it's beneficial to create the 2x2 *with* stakeholders and other nondesigners because the resulting diagram represents diverse points of view. You can extract patterns from the 2x2 to present as unique insights that can be traced back to individual data points.

Learn More
Read *The Power of the 2x2 Matrix: Using 2x2 Thinking to Solve Business Problems and Make Better Decisions* by Alex Lowy and Phil Hood. ISBN 1118008790

METHODS FOR SYNTHESIZING DATA AND DEVELOPING IDEAS
THEORY OF CHANGE MODEL

What is it?

Theory of Change is a tool used to model how short-term changes lead to long-term impacts. It is used primarily in the context of social and humanitarian problems, but it can be used in any context where human efforts intend change (such as problems of engineering, policy, or design). You can think of a Theory of Change as a series of linkages, where one thing leads to another, which leads to another.

The Theory of Change model forces the design team to articulate assumptions. In creating the model, the team designates the inputs—levers—to manipulate and must state how these levers will affect an outcome. The model demands that implied causality be made explicit. The model also identifies linkages between things that are in your control and those that are not. For example, you may have some control over where you place a set of tents for homeless people in the city but little control over existing zoning regulations. The Theory of Change forces you to find a connection between where you place your tents and how policy must be changed.

The Theory of Change also forces the design team to state the nonfinancial value they intend to produce and to link that value to the problem through an intervention. This helps the design team to focus—to say "we are working in support of this, but not that"—and to identify political, social, and systemic constraints.

A Theory of Change is used to define outcomes, and to identify outputs and inputs.

An outcome is the humanitarian value that a team expects to produce, such as minimizing the prevalence of poverty. It is described as a series of changes. Short-term or micro changes might include knowledge, skills, attitudes, and motivations. Medium term—or intermediate—changes may be related to behavior, practice, policy, procedure, activities, and methods. And long-term change affects the environment, social conditions, economic conditions, and political conditions. The outcome describes the "desired state."

To achieve an outcome, you must create outputs, the "who" and "what" of the design intervention. An output describes who is affected—directly and indirectly—by the design team's actions. For example, homeless people may be directly affected by your actions, while the zoning board, neighbors, and politicians are indirectly affected. The output also describes what is produced—the *result* of your product or service—such as the artifacts (physical, digital, or knowledge-based) that are made along the way.

Inputs, sometimes describes as strategies, activities, or interventions, are the things you invest and the product or service that you create. Investments, the resources used to start the process, include time, money, physical resources like buildings or computers, partners, intellectual property, etc. The process of design is a strategic input. The actual product, system, service, activities, interventions, or other "design product" that is made also acts as an input into your Theory of Change because without it, the cycle would not begin.

METHODS FOR SYNTHESIZING DATA AND DEVELOPING IDEAS
THEORY OF CHANGE MODEL, CONTINUED

How do I do it?

To use a Theory of Change, include ethnographic research, meaningful empathy, and a degree of humility, and an insistence that the desired end state be culturally sensitive. In light of "design *with* versus design *for*," build the Theory of Change with your target audience—including the users whom your design will affect.

First, ask, and answer, questions about the *existing* problem. Describe the need, and explain who has it. For example, you might want to help the homeless people in your city, and so you might frame their need as "the homeless people in my city need physical shelter to protect them from the weather." That statement describes the problem, why it's a problem, and whom it affects. But it also makes large-scale assumptions that you must validate. Are you sure homeless people want physical shelters or that they don't already have access to them? Is weather the largest problem they face, or are other problems more pressing? As you gain empathy with your target audience, you can better answer these questions. Recruit people from the target audience as co-designers.

Next, describe the *desired* state. If you are successful, what will the world look like? Also describe the people who benefit and how they benefit. For example, if you successfully provide physical shelter for homeless people, you would answer questions such as these:

- Do all homeless people benefit? Or only those who habituate certain neighborhoods? Only women and children?

- Do the served population have access to shelter that is permanent, or only temporary? And any day, or only when the weather is bad?

- Does the change affect only housing, or does it also address compounding issues, such as economic self-sufficiency, literacy, and self-confidence?

For Example:
Austin Center for Design's Theory of Change

	Education	Company Incubation	Knowledge Creation and Public Dissemination
Activities	Classes are held in theory, methods, and processes of interaction design and social entrepreneurship	Companies receive ongoing mentorship, access to resources (including physical space), and collaborative community during incubation and beta development stages	The public receives access to public lectures, presentations, documents and resources related to social entrepreneurship pedagogy and theory
Outputs	Students gain competency in various aspects of conducting, thinking about, and managing large-scale social problem engagements	Companies scale to a point where they are operationally self-sufficient and engaged in double-bottom-line activities	The public gains awareness of the role of design and social entrepreneurship in mitigating large-scale social problems
Short Term Outcomes	Students demonstrate ability to design in the context of large social and service problems, utilizing empathy, prototyping, and abductive reasoning	Companies demonstrate double-line impact through both quantitative and qualitative metrics	The public demonstrates a shift in values, engaging with more subjective, discursive, and divergent approaches to creative problem solving in the context of social problems
Long Term Outcomes	Students mentor, manage, hire, and train others in the unique process of designing for social impact and change	Additional, non-AC4D companies adopt the cultural and tactical approach taken by incubated companies, advancing the role of "problems worth solving"	The public accepts a designerly perspective as fundamental to tackling large-scale social problems

METHODS FOR SYNTHESIZING DATA AND DEVELOPING IDEAS
THEORY OF CHANGE MODEL, CONTINUED

Also objectively describe the people who may suffer from your change. For example, how do the downtown shop owners and their businesses react to a new homeless center in their areas? Does the center affect tourism; if so, how? Does it change how others who support homeless people do their jobs?

Clearly, you don't know for sure, but you can tell a credible story about the desired situation, and you can continue to refine it over time.

Now define the behaviors that need to change to achieve the outcome. Who needs to change—just the homeless people, or also politicians, voters, the police, and neighbors? Identify each individual or set of constituents and describe and examine the behaviors that must change. Come up with an incentive structure for the necessary behavioral change. What are the rewards, and are they financial, social, or cultural? How will they know about these rewards? Are the rewards part of your design intervention, or do they come as a result of changing attitudes? Also describe the constraints on behavioral change. What roadblocks do you face as you attempt to shift attitudes and behaviors?

Finally, draw the Theory of Change as a model (sometimes called a "logic diagram" or "logic model"). Draw a series of boxes that represent inputs, outputs, and outcomes. Arrows connect the boxes to show how one step leads to another. Inputs—your activities and designed interventions—lead to Outputs—the knowledge and results of your interventions. Outputs lead to Outcomes, the social value you are seeking. This model may contain as few as three steps or as many as a dozen.

At each step, reflect on your contextual research and ethnography. What do you know about the target population that can inform your assumptions? Are you making broad generalizations that you can narrow with further research? What do you know the most about? What do you know the least about?

When should I use it?

You can create a Theory of Change model at the start of a social entrepreneurship engagement, but it will be most useful when some ethnographic data informs the model's creation—when you can claim some degree of expertise over the content. Then continue to refine the model over the course of your work. Stick the model on the wall in your workspace and review it weekly: Have your priorities and goals changed? Have constraints shifted? Has your increasing knowledge shed light on new opportunities or demands?

What is the output, and how can I use it?

The Theory of Change model is a map—a visual illustration of how steps in a process link to one another and how actions in the shape of designed interventions drive change. It shows a chain of events leading from the things you can control the most (your design) to the things you control the least (other people's behaviors).

Learn More

Read the free eBook Theory of Change: A Practical Tool for Action, Results and Learning, by Organizational Research Services.

Created by Ruby Ku and Alex Pappas

HourSchool began as a project about homelessness at Austin Center for Design. We met with homeless people and listened to their stories. The people we met are like you and me, but going through tough times and trying to improve their situations. We found that their biggest problem is perception—both in how society perceives them and how that perception affects how they perceive themselves.

Over and over, homeless people told us that the best part of their day was when they could help others and share what they know—from carpentry and roofing to oil painting and computer skills. Self-actualization, at the top of Maslow's Hierarchy of Needs pyramid, is at the core of what makes us human. It needs to be fulfilled so we can desire to live, not just be able to live. That desire is often what separates people who are chronically homeless from those who are trying to change their situation. And that's where HourSchool diverges from many social-service organizations, including those that provide essential services such as shelter, food, and medical help. They exist on the belief that the bottom layers of Maslow's pyramid must be served before one can move up into social, esteem, and self-actualization needs. But although survival depends on meeting physiological needs, their fulfillment is not enough to lift someone out of homelessness. We combined this belief with our observations of people's enhanced self-esteem when they share their knowledge. These insights led us to focus on people's assets, not their liabilities. For homeless people to feel power to change their situations, we began to look at what they could offer.

The innate need of all of us to feel needed, useful, and part of a community remains true regardless of economic situation and residential status. It applies to anyone who doesn't have outlets to give back and share what they know—the retired folks, the college-educated barista, and those who don't necessarily get to use all of our skills and passions in our day job.

On the skill of starting something

A small team on a start-up venture presents other challenges. The types of expertise—finance, operations, marketing, technical development—that a large firm usually provides were not available in starting our own company. Learning how to create something from scratch had a steep learning curve with inevitable failures and mistakes. Creating social impact through ventures required a sustained focus in an area of passion through rounds of success, failure, and evolution. But being a start-up also conveyed a certain freedom, in that we had no brand, legacy product, or people to protect. Instead, momentum and progress became the most important assets.

On measuring impact

The goal of starting a social enterprise is to make a difference. To know if we were succeeding, we first needed to understand what success means to us, as well as how our definition of success might be similar or different than those of investors and donors. For example, we worked with an organization that provides subsidized housing for people who are transitioning out of homelessness. The organization's donors measure success by the number of classes and number of people attending. However, the organization itself looks to other metrics, such as increases in income, education, community involvement, and length of stay in housing, plus intangible, emotional benefits such as increases in self-esteem and rebuilt relationships. These intangible goals require a different perspective than those that result in quantifiable growth. At the same time, though, growth attracts more funding, attention, and talent—resources to do more with less. The challenge for a social entrepreneur becomes keeping this delicate balance through the various stages of growth.

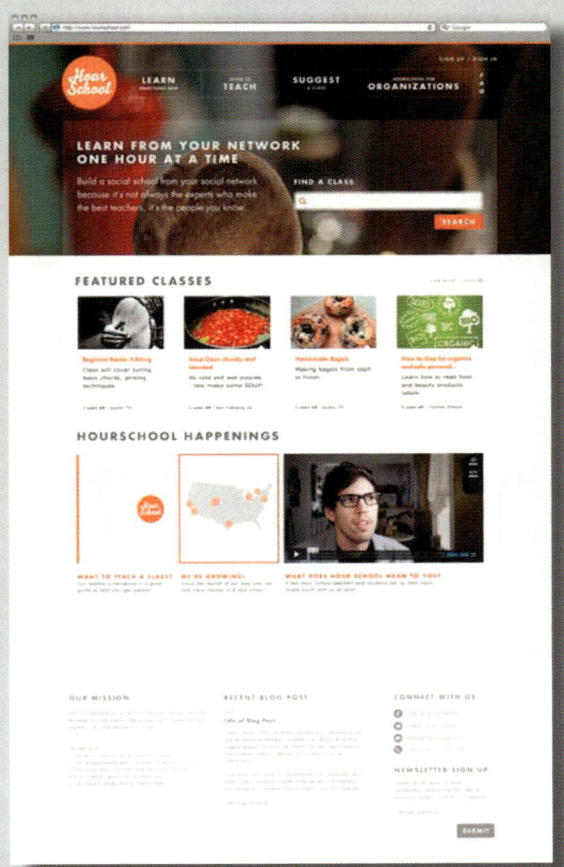

METHODS FOR SYNTHESIZING DATA AND DEVELOPING IDEAS
CONCEPT MAPPING

What is it?

A concept map is a diagram of knowledge that supports meaningful learning through connection forming. [43] Because knowledge is made explicit and tangible—literally, drawn out on a piece of paper—it can provoke collaborative development within a design team.

A concept map shows relationships between elements: typically the people, entities, and artifacts engaged in work, and the way they interact with one another. The map can capture a theoretical idea, a series of political influences, a system of interaction, or the pragmatic steps someone takes to achieve a goal. In all cases, the emphasis is on the externalization of ideas and the shared creation and interpretation of the artifact within a group.

---

43   Novak, Joseph, and Alberto Cañas. "How People Learn." August 29, 2009. http://cmap.ihmc.us/docs/howpeoplelearn.html (accessed November 10, 2011).

How do I do it?

You can produce a concept map by following these steps:

1. Identify the words and phrases that make up the system you are mapping. Extract this language from contextual inquiry or interview transcripts, or free-associate it through brainstorming. To help you identify the language, you might imagine yourself walking through scenarios you've observed; each time you think of a person, item, action, policy, or influence, capture the thought with a tool such as Excel or on a large sheet of paper; a moderately complex domain may have thousands of relevant terms.

2. Identify the most important terms: typically people, groups, or policies. These will serve as containers

METHODS FOR SYNTHESIZING DATA AND DEVELOPING IDEAS
CONCEPT MAPPING, CONTINUED

and "anchoring" elements for the other words and ideas. Write these words in big letters on a large sheet of paper. This is the preliminary concept map.

3. Go back to your long word list, and add words to the map that directly relate to the anchor words. Add the words near their anchors and use lines to connect them. On each line, write the two word's relationship as a verb or sentence.

4. Continue through all of the words. As the map grows, you'll probably run out of room. Start again, redrawing the material in a more cohesive manner. As you do, you might find it helpful to literally cut sections out of the paper and attach them to the next revision.

Use your completed map as a tool. For example, you can compare the "existing state," version of the map with an alternative version that represents the "idealized state," where you introduce new policies, procedures, design ideas or artifacts to solve problems you perceive. Because the map is made up of words, design at this stage is a simple task of adding new language to the map; the difficulties of implementation are, temporarily, removed.

When should I use it?

Use a concept map during and after research to make sense of large amounts of data and to better understand relationships between individual data points. By creating the concept map in a group, your design team will form a shared and collective understanding of a complex system. And because a concept map is easy to understand, it can be used as a primary means of co-design; consider building the concept map with end users.

Refine the map throughout the process of design to a constantly evolving representation of your knowledge and understanding of a system. After each new contextual inquiry, add concepts to the map or revise the relationships between people and artifacts.

What is the output, and how can I use it?
A piece of paper with a lot of words on it, a concept map is typically messy and confusing. Re-create the raw output in a digital tool before you share it with stakeholders.

Learn More
Read *Applied Concept Mapping: Capturing, Analyzing, and Organizing Knowledge* by Brian M. Moon, Robert R. Hoffman, Joseph D. Novak, Alberto J. Cañas. ISBN 1439828601

METHODS FOR SYNTHESIZING DATA AND DEVELOPING IDEAS
SEMANTIC ZOOM

What is it?

Powers of Ten, a 1977 film by Charles and Ray Eames, illustrates the relative nature of things by literally zooming out from a human to the earth, and from the earth to the solar system. The point is simple but powerful: Changing the scale of a problem illustrates new problems, issues, and opportunities, and it allows the designer to recontextualize or reframe the problem. Any problem or situation can be repositioned in a larger or smaller context. For example, zooming out from the homelessness problem shows it as part of a larger story of wealth, opportunity, public policy, and education. We also can zoom *in* on a specific part of homelessness, such as shelters, an individual shelter, a policy enforced in an individual shelter, or a specific person enforcing a specific policy at an individual shelter. Each time we zoom—each time we recast the problem—we see new things, identify new opportunities, and consider a problem from a new perspective.

Everything is embedded in a larger context, and everything has smaller details, so semantic zoom is possible in every situation. And in forcing a semantic zoom, you may realize you don't have the knowledge or expertise to describe the new perspective, so this method can also provoke further research.

How do I do it?

A semantic zoom leverages the concept map—described above—as a base visualization. To produce the various zooms, follow these steps:

1. Start with the concept map, and consider this the base zoom level—"zoom level 0."

2. Back away from the map, literally and figuratively, to consider the broader context in which it exists. What are the large social and political constructs that contain the material? Name these constructs, and write these names close to the existing words.

3. Repeat Step #2, continuing to back away—zoom out—and consider broad context. At each zoom, create a new visual representation of the system.

4. Gradually zoom back in, while focusing on a specific aspect of the original concept map. As you zoom in, boundaries of the map change, forcing you to add details, entities, and actions.

5. After performing several zooms in both directions, consider the results. Which areas were easy to describe, and which were difficult? Did you find yourself making assumptions or guesses about content? The answers indicate the limitations of your knowledge and areas for additional research.

When should I use it?

Use a semantic zoom to see a problem in a new way. This tool is typically useful after you have researched a given aspect of a system enough to understand what you don't know. The semantic zoom calls attention to the most compelling areas for further research.

What is the output, and how can I use it?

The output of a semantic zoom is a series of visualizations of a system. They look just like the concept map, but they can appear in a series and show multiple scales.

METHODS FOR SYNTHESIZING DATA AND DEVELOPING IDEAS
SEMANTIC ZOOM, CONTINUED

Semantic Zoom Level +1

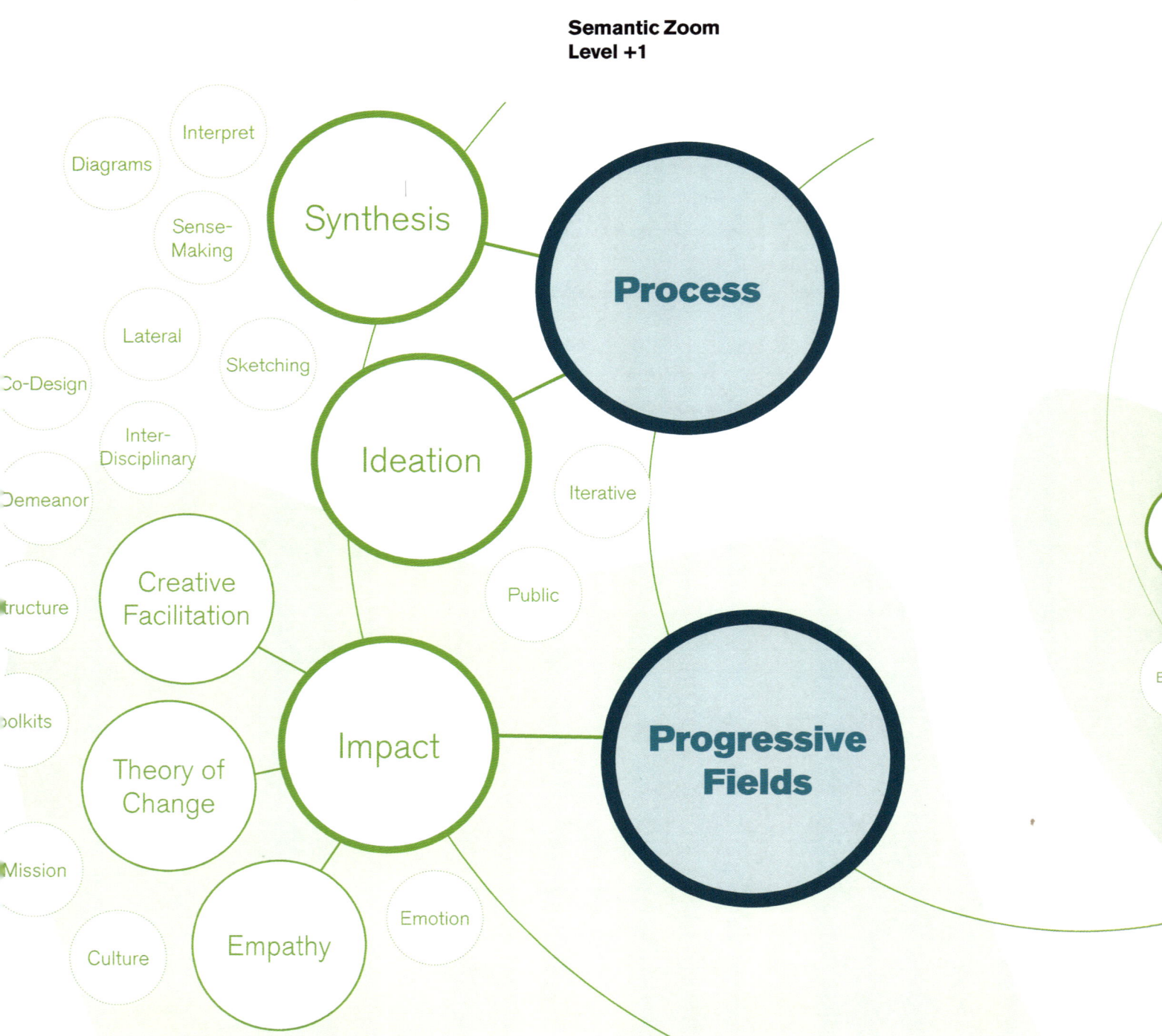

Semantic Zoom Level 0

Semantic Zoom Level -1

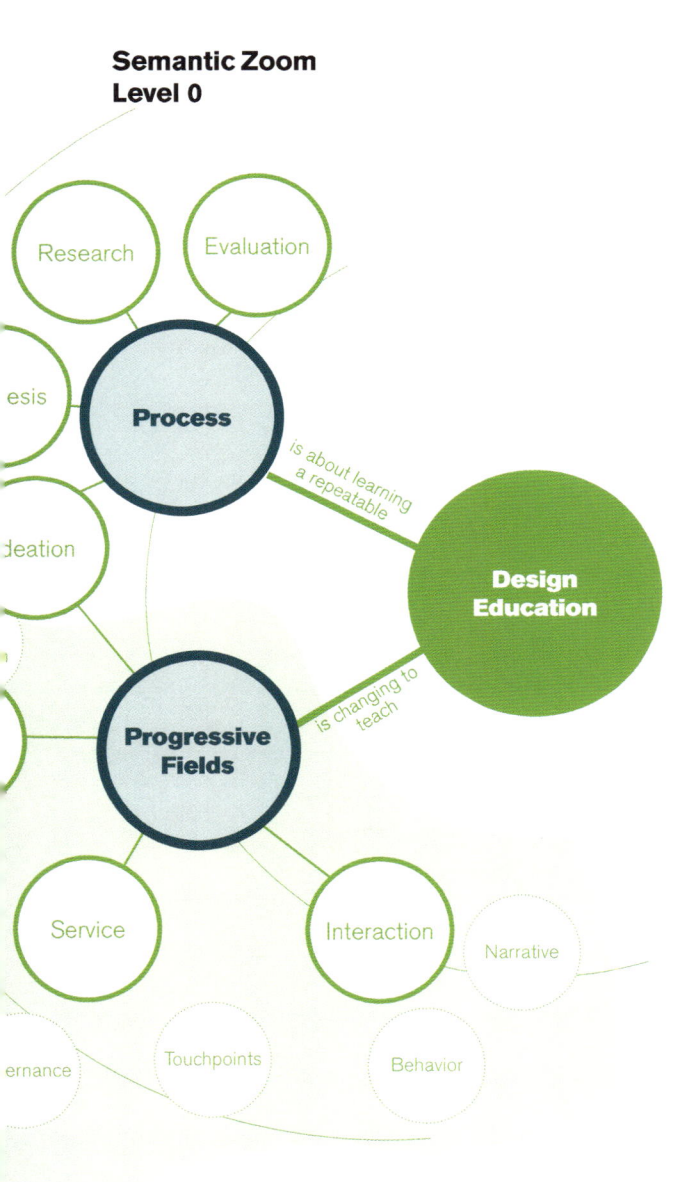

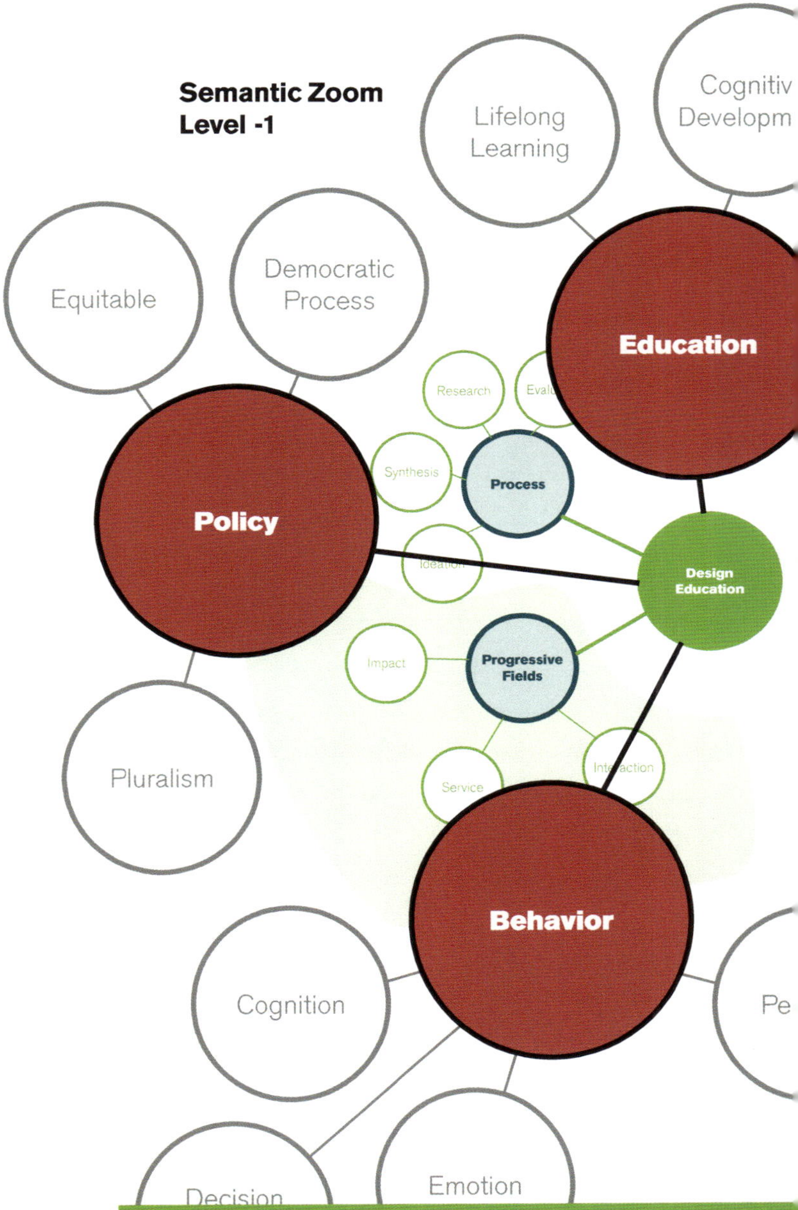

Learn More

Read *Exposing the Magic of Design* by Jon Kolko. ISBN 0199744335

METHODS FOR SYNTHESIZING DATA AND DEVELOPING IDEAS
INSIGHT COMBINATION

What is it?

Insight combination is a method to quickly generate a lot of design ideas and explicitly tie these ideas to contextual research and the cultural nuances of your target audience. Insight combination leverages *forced provocation*—the ability to constantly ask and answer "what if" without fear of critique. Insights from contextual research combine with trends and patterns to form design constraints that drive "what if" questions.

Insight is derived from user research and interpretation. Use the insight as a point of departure for creative ideation. Examples of insights are "Users who take medication seek both privacy and community," and "People who are diagnosed with a disease immediately see the world in a new way."

Trends—changes in technology, social norms, fashion, or politics—typically reflect larger emotional changes in groups or subcultures. Examples are "People are spending more time at home doing inexpensive activities" and "Parents are unaware of their children's online behavior." Again, both trend statements are provocative and unsubstantiated, but they're also derived from personal observation and interactions.

To combine insights with trends, you must methodically examine each one along with each facet of the design problem that has been deemed useful or important. The method actively produces new ideas. Ideas expand and become fleshed out in a nonlinear fashion, jumping over the expected to arrive at the unexpected.

How do I do it?

For best results, combine insights after you conduct contextual research:

1. Identify insights in your transcripts, concept maps, and other research records and tools. An insight starts with something provocative, interesting, unique, or surprising. When you find these things, highlight them and form a "why" question about it: Why did the user do something? Why did a person respond in a certain way? Why is the system set up with certain rules or processes?

   Then answer the *why* question, telling a credible story. The answer usually holds an insight. Frame each insight as a provocative statement of fact, and write it on a yellow note card. Consider using different colors for each area of insight. As a guideline, try to identify approximately 50 insights in every two hours of transcript.

2. Identify trends in politics, television, film, art, food, music, technology, and other cultural aspects; write or draw them on blue note cards.

3. Combine a design trend with an insight at random, mingling the blue and yellow cards. Working quickly with a single insight and a single trend in hand, create a new design idea to use in the context of your design opportunity. What new product, system, or service can you envision that leverages the trend to fulfill the needs represented on the insight? Write or draw the new design idea on a green card. Spend no more than 60 seconds per design idea; the goal is to identify as many ideas as possible, rather than trying to come up with just one good idea.

When should I use it?

Use insight combination to generate ideas to existing problems without attention to constraints. As you learn more about a given topic, you'll become aware of existing domain constraints. Insight combination reminds you that these constraints can be flexible. It also forces you to re-examine what matters most in the topic or domain.

What is the output, and how can I use it?

Insight combination results in hundreds of different design "seeds"—initial, incomplete design ideas that can spawn further ideation and that you can refine into finished design concepts. You can analyze these seeds through various techniques, such as the 2x2 described above, to help identify the most feasible ideas.

Learn More

Read "Abductive Thinking and Sensemaking: The Drivers of Design Synthesis" by Jon Kolko. www.jonkolko.com/writingAbductiveThinking.php

METHODS FOR CREATING NEW DESIGNS
SCENARIO PLANNING

What is it?

A scenario is a story that describes a different way for things to be. You might use it to call attention to a problem or to highlight an opportunity. Scenarios are valuable because they are accessible; nearly anyone from any discipline can read and evaluate a story *on a human level*, without needing deep technical, organizational, or political knowledge.

Scenario Planning is a form of provocative, "what-if" thinking that helps us strategically consider how the world will be different as a result of our actions and efforts. It "attempts to capture the richness and range of possibilities, stimulating decision makers to consider changes they would otherwise ignore. At the same time, it organizes these possibilities into narratives that are easier to grasp than great volumes of data. Above all, however, scenarios are aimed at challenging the prevailing mindset." [44]

In designing for impact, the Scenario Planning method forces the rigorous creation of multiple scenarios and their evaluation and comparison. This rigor provokes designers to investigate alternative end states, to consider the relationship between them, and to identify optimal targets as well as potential constraints and roadblocks.

How do I do it?

Follow these steps:

1. Define your evaluation's scope, including time frame and the major issues you are investigating. Consider starting with a year-long time frame. Although business strategic planning may look at ten years, the reliability of a prediction diminishes with every year projected.

   Then begin to describe the thematic quality of your interest. Are you concerned with increases in crime? The role of policy on the homeless? The nature of sustainable farming? Define the scope as it relates to your project topic.

---

44 Schoemaker, Paul. "Scenario Planning: A Tool for Strategic Thinking." Sloan Management Review, no. Winter (1995): 25.

2. Create a trend table:

Trend	Uncertainties	Stakeholders
Articulate the basic trends that you see affecting your scope. What new companies, products, services, policies, regulations, or people are beginning to play a role in your particular area of focus? List these, one per row.	Describe the uncertainties related to the trend. For example, if you see a trend related to increased federal intervention in a given social issue, uncertainty exists in the staying power of that intervention; if the political party in power is voted out, the trend may reverse.	Describe the stakeholders involved in the issues you are planning around. Be broad in your definition of involvement; try to identify all stakeholders, and describe their roles, interests, and the power or influence they have over the situation.

METHODS FOR CREATING NEW DESIGNS
SCENARIO PLANNING, CONTINUED

3. Combine the details above and look at how they interact. First, create an "ideal scenario," in which everything goes according to plan, and the future plays out exactly as you desire. What is the end state in your time frame? Now, create a "doomsday scenario," in which everything goes wrong. Continue to create scenarios in which your major uncertainties play out in different directions. What happens when a conservative set of policymakers come into power? What about a liberal set?

    When you create scenarios, you are writing stories of how the world will look. Because you are assuming external events, these narratives often take the form of cause-and-effect situations, where an entity does something (launches a new product, creates a new policy) that forces other entities to react.

4. Validate your scenarios by checking for internal consistency. Are your anticipated trends likely to play out in the time frame you identified in #1? What are plausible ways for involved stakeholders to react? To judge that plausibility, consider stakeholders' relative level of risk aversion, based on previous events.

5. Name the scenarios (use short, action-oriented names) so they become tangible points of departure for further research and evaluation. Many proponents of scenario-planning methods suggest using scenarios to form quantitative models that let you adjust financial variables to understand how events play out. For example, today you could create a quantitative financial model that a) includes the actual amount of federal money dedicated to a certain cause that interests you, b) assumes a percentage of that money is dedicated to relevant initiatives, and as a result, c) predicts the amount of spending power a given nonprofit will have for your cause, if it were to agree with your initiatives.

When should I use it?

Use scenario planning in the initial strategic phases of considering a future—at the beginning of the design process. But use it only after contextual research, immersion, and other forms of participation with various stakeholders. Because of the number of assumptions you'll probably make, it's important to have an understanding of the topic and discipline you are engaged in.

What is the output, and how can I use it?

Scenario-planning sessions provide written stories that represent alternative views of the future. These stories can be shared and used as mechanisms for continually evaluating and revising design ideas.

Learn More

Read "Scenario Planning: A Tool for Strategic Thinking" by Paul J. H. Schoemaker.

METHODS FOR CREATING NEW DESIGNS
USE CASES

What is it?

A Use Case is a formal version of a scenario—a story that describes someone using a product, system, or service to achieve a goal. Compared with scenarios, Use Cases embody a much more rigorous approach to storytelling. In addition to one "main path," systems typically include dozens or even hundreds of other paths people can take on their way to accomplishing their goals. Use Cases are intended to capture the breadth of interactions—both normal and uncommon—someone could have with a system. They help engineers and other technical team members to describe functionality requirements and build a system that matches users' needs. Additionally, use cases can feed directly into "test cases": the narrative-based evaluation methods used by software developers to check their code for defects.

Use Cases are written, but are typically accompanied by a diagram of actions and interactions.

How do I do it?

To create Use Cases, consider the users who are involved and their goals. Working from an overview to a detailed and descriptive view, articulate the steps the users will take to achieve their goals. More specifically, follow these steps:

1. List the actors and their roles. What experience can we assume the actors have with both the system and the domain? For example, the actors involved in a homeless shelter service may include the following:

    Nancy, aged 31, is homeless, has a history of depression and anxiety, and has traveled by herself throughout the southern states for the past six years. She sleeps on the streets until the temperature drops below freezing, when she tries to find a place to sleep inside. She carries a bedroll, a mobile phone, and an expired drivers' license; she goes out of her way to carry as little as possible because she has been robbed several times in the last few months. She typically asks for spare change at a busy corner and knows the best hours and sign messages to encourage donations.

    Mitch, aged 44, is a caseworker who has worked at various Dallas homeless facilities since he graduated from college; he received a Master of

Social Work with a focus on housing and the extreme poor. Recently, he has explored technology-based interventions and has introduced web- and mobile-based tools to support the homeless people and the workers that serve them. At night, Mitch is teaching himself database management and programming.

2. Describe the actors' multiple goals. For example, Nancy's goals in using an SMS-based bed finder on a freezing night may include the following:

    *finding a safe place to sleep for the evening
    finding a female-only facility
    finding a quiet, sparsely populated area
    being discreet
    knowing how long it will take to walk to the sleeping location*

    Mitch's goals for the same system are different:

    *providing care to as many people as possible
    knowing how many people the system serves in a month
    knowing why people return or don't return to the shelter after their first experience*

    As is common in life, various actors' goals often conflict. In this case, Nancy's goals for a quiet and discreet bed may be at odds with Mitch's goals to provide shelter to as many people as possible.

3. Create the main narrative that describes a user using the system to achieve a goal. This should describe success, and focus on the most important goals of a given user. As you write the narrative, be sure to include preconditions, technologies, decision points, assumptions, and actions.

    Preconditions define the existing constraints upon the user. These may include previous knowledge, social and political influences, physical and economic context, etc. Technologies describe the systems that support users' ability to achieve their goals. In addition to digital technologies, such as computers or mobile phones, they may also include physical infrastructure (buildings, spaces) and artifacts (objects, forms, brochures, posters).

METHODS FOR CREATING NEW DESIGNS
USE CASES, CONTINUED

Decision points are moments in which the user is forced to do something, often after needing to choose between two or more directions. These actions have impact on the well-being of other people and the actor, so in decision points, designed interventions can drive emotional and intellectual value.

Assumptions describe why a person is acting in a certain way. Assumptions are based on previous knowledge, the current situation, and various external influences. Assumptions should be credible and should consider emotional, social, economic and political influences, and not just knowledge, as people may act irrationally because of the way they feel.

Actions should be written at a broad level ("Mitch placed a call to Fred") rather than a detailed interaction level ("Mitch pressed the 2 button, then the 4 button…").

4. Craft supporting Use Cases that relate to subgoals, alternative goals, and related goals.

5. Continually refine multiple Use Cases in a design to ensure they support one another. Combine smaller Use Cases or break out cases that can stand on their own.

In writing Use Cases, avoid describing the medium of the solution. For example, if the user is going to be using software, avoid the temptation to describe buttons, labels, and other widgets, for two reasons: This level of specificity creates artificial constraints, which are desired at later phases in the project, but limiting to creativity at this early phase. It also tends to "make the Use Cases long, hard to read, and brittle." [45]

---

45 Cockburn, Alistair. "Use Cases, ten years later." STQE magazine, 2002. http://alistair.cockburn.us/Use+cases,+ten+years+later (accessed October 1, 2011)

When should I use it?
Create Use Cases as an explicit way to move from research and opportunity-finding to designing; Use Cases begin to define the solution. They can be created alongside storyboards or can leverage storyboards as a point of departure. The process of creating Use Cases often highlights areas of incomplete research.

What is the output, and how can I use it?
The output of a cohesive Use Case writing exercise is a series of stories that define the breadth of the system to be designed. Use Cases also act as input into more detailed and pragmatic design artifacts, such as sketches, wireframes, information architecture diagrams, and service design blueprints.

Learn More
Read *Writing Effective Use Cases* by Alistair Cockburn. ISBN 0201702258

METHODS FOR CREATING NEW DESIGNS
STORYBOARD

1

Jim is fed up at his job and is thinking that it's time for a career change.

2

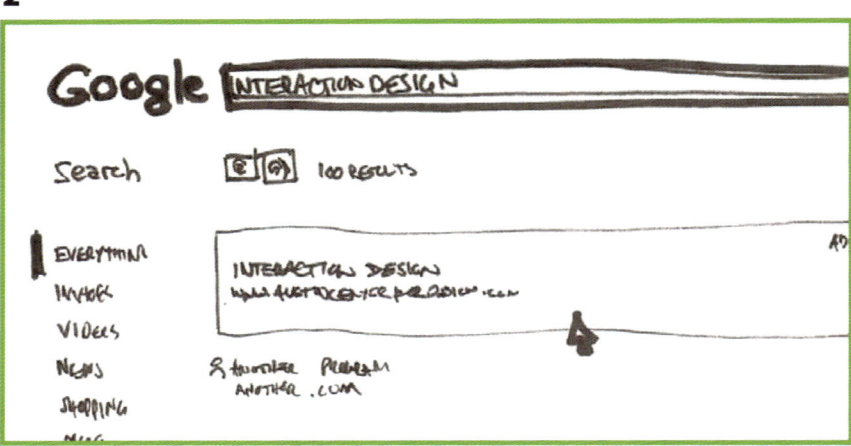

As he googles around, he learns about interaction design, and sees a sponsored link for Austin Center for Design.

What is it?

A storyboard is a visual representation of a scenario. Much like a comic strip, a storyboard combines multiple elements into a visual narrative. These elements include the following:

- scenes: The storyboard contextualizes events in their environment, showing the physical, geographic, or cultural backdrop that helps dictate how people respond to those events.

- actors: The storyboard represents different stakeholders in a situation and how they'll act according to their character "type." For example, someone in an authoritative position will credibly dictate strategy or large-scale direction.

- products: The storyboard embeds products—both physical and digital—into the context and illustrates how actors respond to using them. For example, to illustrate a problem scenario, you could include tiny representations of actors

3

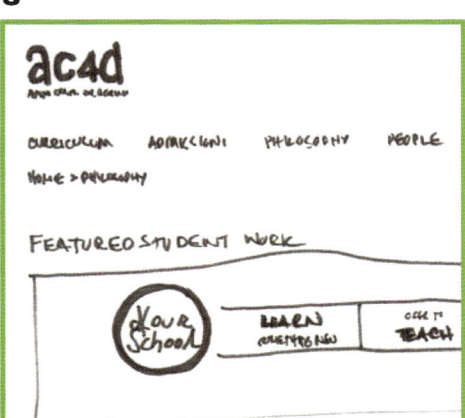

He explores the site, and learns about some of the previous projects.

4

He wants to learn more, and sees the link to chat with an alumni on the phone. He gives it a try.

5

He's connected with Chap Ambrose, an alumni. They talk about the program together.

frustrated by broken products; to illustrate a future scenario of success, you would show tiny happy actors using functional products.

- services and policies: The storyboard also describes the existing service infrastructure—the rules, policies, and guidelines that determine how people act and how they respond to different events.

Because of the storyboard's visual quality, the tool is compelling, evocative, and easy to understand—making it ideal for collaborative design efforts with nondesigners or a nontechnical audience.

METHODS FOR CREATING NEW DESIGNS
STORYBOARD, CONTINUED

How do I do it?

1. Read through the narrative you created in scenario planning (above) to determine the best direction for the storyboard.

2. Create an empty storyboard by drawing a series of 4" squares in a long, horizontal strip. Use a large sheet of paper; newsprint, sold in rolls, works well.

3. Under each square, write one sentence from your narrative.

4. In each square, sketch the sentence. Because this is a generative activity, the focus should be on the quality of the idea, not necessarily the quality of the visualization.

As you sketch the sentence, consider these key points:

What actions are plausible, given actors' circumstance, background, technical acumen, incentive structure, and interest in the topic? For example, your scenario would not depict an actor who has no technical skills as understanding how to use a complex software program the first time he encounters it.

What products, services, systems, and other artifacts are being introduced? Use the storyboard to emphasize what these items look like.

When you show a product, draw it big enough to fill the square. By sketching the product as large as possible, you are beginning to make implicit design decisions, which help minimize the difficulty in further design iterations. For example, if a user encounters a piece of computer software, treat the square as the monitor, and draw what the user would see on it. But even the full square isn't big enough for tiny details, so you'll be forced to simplify user-interface elements rather than rendering them perfectly.

To show an exchange of information, goods, policies, or decisions between two people, include both people in the square. If the people are in different physical locations, use a horizontal line to divide the square in two. If more than two people are sitting around a table, show as many of them as you can. By visualizing these interactions, you begin to establish the collaborative and workflow constraints around your solution.

Each time you introduce a product, service, system, and other artifact, add visual clarity to that element by increasing the line weight or adding more detail to the sketch.

When should I use it?

Use a storyboard as a bridge between high-level design ideas and preliminary product artifacts (such as wireframes, concept sketches, service blueprints, etc.). Typically, a storyboard is informed by research and builds on existing design concepts and inspiration, so it can be used once the design team has identified the "big idea," a compelling design-driven intervention.

What is the output, and how can I use it?

The output of a storyboard is a tangible representation of a story's words and ideas.

Learn More

Read *Exploring Storyboarding* (Design Exploration Series) by Wendy Tumminello. ISBN 1401827152

METHODS FOR CREATING NEW DESIGNS
JOURNEY MAP

What is it?

Our interactions with a particular subject or system occur over time; at some point, we're novices, and as we use a system or have an experience, we gain knowledge and understanding. These interactions over time indicate opportunities for critical designed interventions to help steer tenuous or precarious behavior. For example, when people are afflicted by a difficult disease, they may go through several large phases:

- unawareness, in which they don't know they have the disease.

- awareness, in which they've learned they have the disease but have not yet taken any course of action.

- action, in which they've begun treatment.

- evaluation, in which they examine whether the treatment is working.

The phases are hardly as discrete as described above because each phase is fraught with emotion, difficult decisions to be made, and social consequences. A journey map is a visualization of these actions, emotions, and decisions. It describes how people interact over time and how designed systems support or hinder intellectual and emotional progress. It also identifies areas of opportunity for design-led system changes, as well as key areas of success. Because the journey map is created early in the design process, it can help define what should be designed.

How do I do it?

1. Identify and define the *journey qualities* of the situation you hope to examine. You may go through several iterations of the map before you identify the correct qualities, so it's often easier to start with the following typical ones and revise later:

people involved
processes used
technologies used
major decisions encountered
primary emotions evoked

The qualities you choose become the labels for the y axis of the map.

2. Identify a single moment: a research-derived moment you know the most about. Consider this moment to be a phase. Name it; you might call it "Normal Situation" or "Everyday Situation." On the case of a person encountering a disease, the name might be "Normal Care" or "Treating a Disease." Write the name on the x axis of the map.

3. Write the journey qualities for this phase and their components in a table. For example:

4. Identify the phase directly before the "everyday situation." For example, you might identify the phase before "Normal Care" as "New Patient." Fill in the details for this phase:

	Normal Care
People Involved	Doctor, nurse, loved ones
Processes Used	Daily pill regiment, physical therapy, treatment diary
Technology Used	Calendar, pills
Major Decisions Encountered	To continue treatment, how to pay, how to treat symptoms
Primary Emotions Evoked	Resigned, tedious

	New Patient	Normal Care
People Involved	Doctor, nurse, loved ones, insurance company	Doctor, nurse, loved ones
Processes Used	MRI, blood test	Daily pill regiment, physical therapy, treatment diary
Technology Used	MRI, calendar, pills, drug-intervention chart	Calendar, pills
Major Decisions Encountered	To begin treatment, drug benefits vs. side effects tradeoff	To continue treatment, how to pay, how to treat symptoms
Primary Emotions Evoked	Scared, anxiety	Resigned, tedious

METHODS FOR CREATING NEW DESIGNS
JOURNEY MAP, CONTINUED

	No Diagnosis	New Patient	Normal Care	Deviant Case
People Involved	Loved ones, no-one (potentially hidden)	Doctor, nurse, loved ones, insurance company	Doctor, nurse, loved ones	Doctor, nurse, loved ones
Processes Used	None, self-care	MRI, blood test	Daily pill regiment, physical therapy, treatment diary	Emergency service
Technology Used	Over-the-counter medicine, internet research	MRI, calendar, pills, drug-intervention chart	Calendar, pills	Ambulance, IV
Major Decisions Encountered	To visit the doctor, potential costs incurred, better not knowing	To begin treatment, drug benefits vs. side effects tradeoff	To continue treatment, how to pay, how to treat symptoms	Future avoidance, cost and payment, insurance premiums
Primary Emotions Evoked	Scared, anxiety, annoyance	Scared, anxiety	Resigned, tedious	Scared, embarrassed

5. Continue to look back in time, as far as is relevant. At each step back, name the phase, make a new column for it, and fill it in.

6. Repeat the process moving forward in time. What will happen to the patient? A journey map can capture the idealized state, the negative/problem state, or both, so you could continue to examine what might happen if the patient's medical treatment fails or symptoms change.

7. Critically examine the completed journey map from the following perspectives:

    Are the initial journey qualities correct?
    Are the mapped phases correct?
    Are there gaps in your research or understanding?

    Use the map as a point of departure for further research, and continue to revise it.

When should I use it?
Use a journey map throughout the process of research and synthesis to identify ways to make a service more effective, pleasurable, or useful.

What is the output, and how can I use it?
The output of a journey map is a visualization of how time plays a role in service offerings, and can be used to provoke further discussion or illustrate areas where more research can be done.

Learn More
Read "The Value of Customer Journey Maps: A UX Designer's Personal Journey" by Joel Flom
www.uxmatters.com/mt/archives/2011/09/the-value-of-customer-journey-maps-a-ux-designers-personal-journey.php

METHODS FOR CREATING NEW DESIGNS
BODYSTORMING

What is it?

While designers typically embrace contextual research to inform design, most design is accomplished at a design studio or office. Bodystorming uproots the process by placing creative design activities in an environment like the one that the design will change. The method places primary importance on context, making it easier for designers to gain understanding and empathy with users. When in context, designers can observe behavior; what's more, they can participate in situations, act out roles, and transform themselves into members of the community being served. Bodystorming offers designers three primary benefits:

- It creates an equitable relationship between the designers and design research participants, driving "design *with*"-style solutions. Users become members of the design team; they can critique design ideas, and they are privy to design decisions that will ultimately influence their work and life.

- It allows designers to witness actual behavior, rather than summary or staged behavior. By embedding the creative process in the context of work or play, designers are literally surrounded by actual events, behaviors, triggers, and problems, so they can better understand workflow inefficiencies, workarounds, and other areas for improvement.

- It raises awareness of subtle influences on a given circumstance. Participants may leverage tacit knowledge in their day-to-day activities but may be unaware of their own capabilities. Or, as is common, power relationships, such as that of a boss/subordinate, may influence a situation. Bodystorming reveals these nuances, so designers can better understand how they support or hinder work.

How do I do it?

Bodystorming is deceptively simple: Uproot your design team and drop them in the context of work.

First, identify the location of the context of work and consider the larger ecosystem of a given interaction. For example, if you are designing a transportation system for homeless people, you might identify several potential sites, such as a bus station, a bus, a homeless shelter, and a government office. Consider the accessibility of a given population and examine the site through two lenses:

physical accessibility: You probably won't be able to conduct design research activities in a mission-critical environment, such as an operating room or a trauma center, so you may need to identify the next best location (the waiting room, for example).

social accessibility: Your presence also may not be appropriate in other settings, such as those that need intimate privacy like a case worker engaging with a victim of domestic abuse. In these cases, too, move the team to the next best location.

Next, form a relationship with the stakeholders of each site articulating what you are doing and why you are doing it. Consider the relationship through these two lenses:

cognitive accessibility: Some participant groups will require the facilitator to have years of experience and deep empathy to relate to users. For example, if you are working in the context of drug addiction, it's cognitively inaccessible if your team struggles to understand how the addicted mind makes decisions. In such a case, you would need to add a drug-addiction expert to your design team.[46]

ethical accessibility: Especially when you work with vulnerable populations, such as children or homeless people, examine the ethical implications of before you engage in bodystorming. You'll need to learn how to avoid even unintentional coercion.

Finally, establish your design studio at the bodystorming location. Bring all of the things you normally use to do your work. At every opportunity, engage users and stakeholders in the work you're doing, in order to validate your ideas and receive a non-designer viewpoint.

When should I use it?
Use bodystorming to understand situations that are outside of your comfort zone and set of experiences. Keep your design studio in the unique context for the duration of the project.

What is the output, and how can I use it?
It includes the output of the other design methods: scenarios, diagrams, sketches, and other artifacts. But with this method, you'll generate these items with a deeper understanding and respect for the culture in which your design will ultimately be used.

[46] Oulasvirta, Antti, Esko Kurvinen, and Tomi Kankainen. "Understanding Contexts by Being There: Case Studies in bodystorming." Pers Ubiquit Comput, 2002: 125-134.

Learn More
"Understanding Contexts by Being There: Case Studies in Bodystorming" by Antti Oulasvirta, Esko Kurvinen, Tomi Kankainen.

METHODS FOR CREATING NEW DESIGNS
SERVICE BLUEPRINT

What is it?

In its formal definition, a service is a value exchange between two or more people that occurs over time and across multiple touchpoints, including products, places, digital systems, and all forms of media. A service blueprint maps these touchpoints and describes how their tangible and intangible qualities affect how people feel and how much value they receive.

How do I do it?

Creating a service blueprint requires you to think of a service from the perspectives of both the recipient and the provider.

1. Think about the service process. Describe the value that the recipient (or customer, or user) will receive *if the service is provided successfully*. For example, a hospital service may be "A patient's trauma is fixed or repaired."

2. Service value is usually hierarchical. Working from service completion to inception, list any service goals that support the ultimate goal along the way.

For example, the hierarchy of the hospital example might look like this

- A patient's trauma is fixed or repaired
- A patient's family knows the status of the patient after surgery
- A patient's family is able to locate the patient
- A patient's family understands where to park
- An ambulance clearly knows where to bring a patient
- A patient's family is able to call for and secure an ambulance

3. Consider whether you are missing items between the goal elements. For example, when the family arrives at the hospital, are there multiple buildings? Is there a guard or information booth that greets them? Do they need to pay for parking? How do they pay? Add these to the list. Arrange the goals and steps in a visual timeline. Label the timeline from the perspective of the user.

4. Consider each timeline element from the perspective of the service provider (or providers, as in the hospital example). For example, when the patient's family calls for an ambulance, what is the experience of the service provider? Who answers the call? How does it get routed? What information is collected and passed from person to person? If you don't know, you'll need to find out. Write these elements on the map. Add a new row for any new individual or group. A blueprint may have as few as four rows or as many as dozens, depending of the complexity of the service.

You need to distinguish between interactions that users are aware of and those that are invisible to the user, such as the use of payroll or finance systems, complex forms, or highly technical language, or the need for training. Don't let these off-stage interactions become visible to users because they introduce anxiety or unnecessary complexity and may serve to reduce users' trust or confidence in the system.

5. Consider the transaction points—the handoffs—between the user and the service providers. What artifacts are used to support these exchanges? Is information… written on a piece of paper? …entered into a computer system? …spoken? Show these handoffs on the map by putting a symbol of the artifact between symbols of the people. These handoffs describe the touchpoints of the service. Along with written policies and procedures, these touchpoints dictate how people will use, experience, and feel about your service, so, ultimately, they will describe success or failure.

When should I use it?

Use a service blueprint when you are designing a new system or service to help you understand the various people involved and the necessary touchpoints you need to design. You can also use it to map an existing service, identify and articulate the problems and breakdowns, and propose solutions or touchpoint changes. And a digital product with multiple touchpoints (used in person and on a mobile phone and a computer) is opportune for service blueprinting. Use the method to ensure users' ability to access the information they need and desire on multiple platforms and in a way that makes sense to them.

METHODS FOR CREATING NEW DESIGNS
SERVICE BLUEPRINT, CONTINUED

What is the output, and how can I use it?

A service blueprint is a detailed map of how a series of interactions plays out over time. The output is a visual representation of these interactions. It can be used to present a complicated system, to call attention to areas that need improvement, to define areas for more research, or to drive collaborative consensus.

Student Actions

 Explore
Discover design and social entrepreneurship; learn about Austin Center for Design; explore faculty, students, projects

 Apply
Fill out an application for admission to AC4D

 Determine & Pay
Learn of acceptance or rejection from the program

Pay Tuition

Service Actions, Visible

Manage website content

Advertise availability of application

Send acceptance and rejection letters

Social Media

Scholarly Material

Service Actions, Hidden

Curriculum Development

Candidate Evaluation

Candidate Determination

Orient
Attend our Design for Impact Bootcamp Orientation session, held over three days

Attend Class
Attend 440 course hours of class, in methods, theory, and practice; gain knowledge and experience

Graduate
Graduate from the program, displaying competence in a series of outcomes

Incubate
Continue incubating and developing the company that presents a theory of change

---

Conduct orientation session

Hold classes

Conduct graduation ceremony and dinner

Provide space for companies

Mentor students

Mentor founders

Critique and evaluate work

Promote companies

Orientation Planning

Course Assessment

Graduation Preparation

Faculty Development

Student Evaluation

Learn More
Read "Designing Services That Deliver" by Lynn Shostack.

METHODS FOR PLANNING A BUSINESS
REVENUE AND EXPENSE WORKSHEET

What is it?

Designing in the context of wicked problems requires a long-term, interdisciplinary mindset. An organization that focuses on them needs to exist for years before it can begin to truly claim to realize the impact of their work. Running a company successfully for years requires financial acumen and operational self-sufficiency, so these become fundamental principles for social entrepreneurship.

All forms of financial worksheets track money coming into the business and money flowing out of the business, and determine the difference. A revenue and expense worksheet is used to understand, track, and strategically plan a company's financial stability. It tracks revenue, profit, and expenses, and helps you determine how much you can afford to pay in salaries, how many employees you can afford to support at any given time, and how much you might charge for your services.

How do I do it?

Use the worksheet below to gain a broad view of your finances. (Note that it doesn't include things like tax breaks or other more advanced forms of financial reporting and planning). To fill out the worksheet, start by identifying the major expenses your company incurs. These usually include the following:

- salaries: How much will you pay yourself and everyone else that works with and for you? List these on a monthly basis.

- physical space: Do you need to rent a facility? How much is monthly rent?

- equipment, such as laptops or projectors.

- utilities, such as internet access.

- research costs, such as compensation for participants

Now identify the repeating revenue from expected sales. How much can you charge for your product or service? For example, will people be willing to pay $9.99 a month? $12.99? $19.99? How do you know? And, how big is your entire market? Be conservative when you estimate it because not everyone is a likely candidate for your product. For example, if you define your market as "U.S. college students," you might estimate its size as 30 million. What percentage of this market will be aware—through advertising, marketing, and word of mouth—that your product exists? And what percentage of the people who are aware of your product will actually buy it? An appropriate estimate for a consumer product at a low price point is 5%. So if 5% of 30,000 people buy, you've made 1,500 sales.

You've identified your monthly "revenue upside"—the most revenue you can expect to bring in each month from that revenue stream.

Now identify other sources of revenue, and map the repeating revenue on a monthly basis:

- Consider seed or initial funding. Did you and each of your partners add some amount of money? Have you raised any grant or venture capital?

- Project how your monthly revenue will change as you reach more people through your successes.

You've now established a framework for thinking about revenue and expenses. You know how much you expect to pay per month as expenses, and you can anticipate what you will bring in each month in revenue.

	January
Monthly Starting Balance	$60,000
Revenue	
Projected number of sales	5
Revenue from sales	$25
Total Revenue:	**$25**
Expenses	
Salaries	$4,500
Equipment	-
Service Fees (hosting, etc - usually a percentage of total revenue)	$1
Utilities (include heat, A/C, internet)	$200
Office Space / Rent / Parking	$600
Legal	$500
Travel	-
Marketing	-
Healthcare	-
Insurance	-
Misc	$100
Total Expenses:	**$5,901**
Monthly Profit / Loss	($5,876)
Monthly Ending Balance	$54,123
Total Users Served	5
Income Per User Served	($1,175)

METHODS FOR PLANNING A BUSINESS
REVENUE AND EXPENSE WORKSHEET, CONTINUED

Assumptions

This worksheet makes the following assumptions:

3 employees, each making $1,500 per month, have each contributed $20,000 in seed funding

There are no equipment costs

A service is offered at $5 per month, per customer

The total market size is 250,000 people

During June, 5% of that market size is reached through advertising (12,500 people), and 2% of those reached through advertising transact (250 people)

	Jan	Feb	Mar	Apr	May
Monthly Starting Balance	$60,000	$54,123	$48,842	$43,680	$38,636
Revenue					
Projected number of sales	5	25	50	75	100
Revenue from sales	$25	$125	$250	$375	$500
Total Revenue:	**$25**	**$125**	**$250**	**$375**	**$500**
Expenses					
Salaries	$4,500	$4,500	$4,500	$4,500	$4,500
Equipment	-	-	-	-	-
Service Fees (hosting, etc - usually a percentage of total revenue)	$1	$6	$13	$19	$25
Utilities (include heat, A/C, internet)	$200	$200	$200	$200	$200
Office Space / Rent / Parking	$600	$600	$600	$600	$600
Legal	$500	-	-	-	-
Travel	-	-	-	-	-
Marketing	-	-	-	-	-
Healthcare	-	-	-	-	-
Insurance	-	-	-	-	-
Misc	$100	$100	$100	$100	$100
Total Expenses:	**$5,901**	**$5,406**	**$5,413**	**$5,419**	**$5,425**
Monthly Profit / Loss	($5,876)	($5,281)	($5,163)	($5,044)	($4,925)
Monthly Ending Balance	$54,123	$48,842	$43,680	$38,636	$33,711
Total Users Served	5	25	50	75	100
Income Per User Served	($1,175)	($211)	($103)	($67)	($49)

Note that, for simplification purposes, no taxes are accounted for in this model.

	Jun	Jul	Aug	Sep
	$33,711	$29,199	$25,774	$24,724
	250	500	1000	2000
	$1,250	$2,500	$5,000	$10,000
	$1,250	**$2,500**	**$5,000**	**$10,000**
	$4,500	$4,500	$4,500	$4,500
	-	-	-	-
	$63	$125	$250	$500
	$200	$200	$200	$200
	$600	$600	$600	$600
	-	-	-	-
	-	-	-	-
	$300	$400	$400	$400
	-	-	-	-
	-	-	-	-
	$100	$100	$100	$100
	$5,763	**$5,925**	**$6,050**	**$6,300**
	($4,513)	($3,425)	($1,050)	$3,700
	$29,199	$25,774	$24,724	$28,424
	250	500	1000	2000
	($18.05)	($6.85)	($1.05)	$1.85

Download an Excel version at www.wickedproblems.com/d/worksheet1.xlsx

When should I use it?

Create an initial revenue and expense worksheet when you understand who your target market is and what your product or service is. Then continue to revise and refine this model as you operate your business. You'll probably find that your initial estimates were wrong, and you'll be able to replace them with actual historic transactional data to better inform and predict the future of your business.

What is the output, and how can I use it?

The most obvious output of the revenue and expense worksheet is a single per-month profit-and-loss figure—an indication of profitability. But the worksheet provides more useful data than just this simple number. For example, the worksheet defines expectations in served users and reached populations to begin to illustrate your expectations of growth and publicity. It also defines your assumptions about a given market's size, and—over time—tells you whether you were correct. And it helps you realize how changes in product and service pricing can support or hinder your company's operational self-sufficiency.

Learn More

A thorough description of forecasting revenue is available at www.entrepreneur.com/article/76418

METHODS FOR PLANNING A BUSINESS
3-TIER SUBSIDY WORKSHEET

What is it?

The triple-tiered subsidy worksheet extends the revenue and expense worksheet (described above) to include basic financial information related to additional revenue streams. A combined focus on profitability and social impact often implies that a given service's *users* are not the same as its *payers*. So the payers often subsidize the service to nonpaying users. This subsidy can take many forms; one example is the three-tiered approach, where social entrepreneurs offer a free product, a product targeted at paying consumers, and a product targeted at large businesses, all leveraging the same core design innovation.

In this model, entrepreneurs may create a service providing immense social value, and give it away to those in need. This is the first tier of the model—the "social purchase." It's a purchase that is subsidized—the product is offered at low cost or for free to people who meet certain requirements. This may be the best way to get the product into an NGO or a nonprofit or to influence decisions within local government or supporting agencies.

Simultaneously, entrepreneurs may supplement, augment, or redirect the product or service for sale to "regular" paying consumers. This is the second tier of the model. The internet makes it easy to target consumers, and the sheer quantity of consumers may tempt you to reach out to this group as a main audience.

The third tier of the model provides the major financial base, as it targets the enterprise. "Enterprise" typically refers to large institutions that can distribute the product to thousands of users, often paying on a per-user model. "Enterprise customers" generally implies a medium or large-size business that buys a software product, on a monthly basis, for staff members. A company may purchase 100 "seats" of a product, meaning that 100 different people can use the product at any given time. An enterprise customer has different needs than a commercial consumer, and you'll want to leverage these differences:

- Decision-makers in an enterprise sale are often not end users. They may be in purchasing, information technology, or human resources.

- The amount of time it takes to sell software or service is much longer when engaging with an enterprise customer. An enterprise sales cycle can last six months or a year. That's often because more people need to be involved in the decision-making process, and the purchasers may not have the budgetary authority to sign off on the purchase themselves.

- The amount of money spent in an enterprise sale is much larger than in a consumer sale. At one time, an enterprise may purchase 1000 seats of a piece of software, at $10/seat/month.

When used successfully, the triple-tiered subsidy model provides the following benefits:

- Large, enterprise customers provide the bulk of incoming revenue.

- Consumer purchases create less revenue but more volume, so they increase the awareness of your company

- Both enterprise and consumer purchases subsidize your ability to provide the product for free to people who cannot afford it.

But the model also presents challenges. Perhaps the biggest one is this: To implement a three-tiered subsidy model, a product needs to offer a single platform-based value proposition across all three audiences, yet retain a common core.

How do I do it?

Fill out the revenue and expense worksheet as described above. But in addition to defining and predicting market sizes and expectations for consumer behavior, also do so for enterprise and social purchases. Consider that both groups will require much more time and attention, so appropriately plan your staffing needs and selling time.

METHODS FOR PLANNING A BUSINESS
3-TIER SUBSIDY WORKSHEET, CONTINUED

Assumptions

This worksheet makes the same assumptions as in the revenue and expense worksheet, and adds these:

Enterprise service is offered at the same price, $5 per month, per user

Separate (additional) marketing efforts are required to attract enterprise customers

"Social sales" describe the subsidized population

	Jan	Feb	Mar	Apr	May
Monthly Starting Balance	$60,000	$54,123	$48,842	$43,680	$38,636
Revenue					
Number of consumer sales	5	25	50	75	100
Revenue from consumer sales	$25	$125	$250	$375	$500
Number of enterprise sales	0	0	0	0	0
Revenue from enterprise sales	$0	$0	$0	$0	$0
Number of social sales	5	25	50	75	100
Revenue from social sales	$0	$0	$0	$0	$0
Total Revenue:	**$25**	**$125**	**$250**	**$375**	**$500**
Expenses					
Salaries	$4,500	$4,500	$4,500	$4,500	$4,500
Equipment	-	-	-	-	-
Service Fees (hosting, etc - usually a percentage of total revenue)	$1	$6	$13	$19	$25
Utilities (include heat, A/C, internet)	$200	$200	$200	$200	$200
Office Space / Rent / Parking	$600	$600	$600	$600	$600
Legal	$500	-	-	-	-
Travel	-	-	-	-	-
Marketing	-	-	-	-	-
Healthcare	-	-	-	-	-
Insurance	-	-	-	-	-
Misc	$100	$100	$100	$100	$100
Total Expenses:	**$5,901**	**$5,406**	**$5,413**	**$5,419**	**$5,425**
Monthly Profit / Loss	($5,876)	($5,281)	($5,163)	($5,044)	($4,925)
Monthly Ending Balance	$54,123	$48,842	$43,680	$38,636	$33,711
Total Users Served	10	50	100	150	200
Income Per User Served	($587)	($105)	($52)	($34)	($24)

Note that, for simplification purposes, no taxes are accounted for in this model.

	Jun	Jul	Aug	Sep
	$33,711	$28,999	$26,874	$28,524
	250	500	1000	2000
	$1,250	$2,500	$5,000	$10,000
	0	100	200	300
	$0	$2,000	$4,000	$6,000
	250	500	1000	2000
	$0	$0	$0	$0
	$1,250	**$4,500**	**$9,000**	**$16,000**
	$4,500	$4,500	$4,500	$4,500
	-	-	-	-
	$63	$225	$450	$800
	$200	$200	$200	$200
	$600	$600	$600	$600
	-	-	-	-
	-	-	-	-
	$500	$1,000	$1,500	$2,000
	-	-	-	-
	-	-	-	-
	$100	$100	$100	$100
	$5,963	**$6,625**	**$7,350**	**$8,200**
	($4,713)	($2,125)	$1,650	$7,800
	$28,999	$26,874	$28,524	$36,324
	500	1100	2200	4300
	($9.43)	($1.93)	$0.75	$1.81

Download an Excel version at www.wickedproblems.com/d/worksheet2.xlsx

When should I use it?

Use the triple-tiered subsidy worksheet when you have a core product offering that can easily extend into the enterprise or a nonprofit context. For example, if you've developed financial-management software for individuals, slightly different features and price points may make it easily extend to helping *businesses* do the same.

What is the output, and how can I use it?

The output is a digital worksheet that can be easily changed as your assumptions and business model change. This worksheet results in an understanding and indication of how multiple user groups can be served with the same or similar product offerings at various price points. The model provides insight into the amount of time necessary to achieve the financial and broad impact desired.

Learn More

Learning about subsidies in other contexts can help explain how you might be able to apply them in your business; explore how government subsidies work at www.earthtrack.net/subsidy-primer

METHODS FOR PLANNING A BUSINESS
PRODUCT AND FEATURE ROADMAP

What is it?

When you develop a product, you may be tempted to include a lot of features and functions to boost the product's perceived value. But if you try to include too many capabilities at once, you'll run into several problems:

- You'll delay the launch of your product. Each time you add something, you'll need to design it, test it, and understand how it changes the holistic feeling of your product or service—all of which takes time.

- You'll increase the complexity of your product idea. In your users' minds, each new capability competes with existing capabilities, making it difficult to understand how things work or predict how your creation provides value.

- You'll become overwhelmed by the amount of work and may end up abandoning the idea in its entirety.

A product and feature roadmap helps to prevent such problems. It describes the elements that make up a given product and illustrates how the product will grow over time. That means it also manages the complexity of new features and capabilities and can help you strategically change your product over time without delaying important pilot tests, releases, or launches. The roadmap is a timeline of your product, describing how it changes with the addition or subtraction of various capabilities.

How do I do it?

First, list your product's capabilities: the set of features that support your users in achieving their goals and produce your desired value and social impact. Give them names that clearly identify the unique elements. For example, you may be designing a SMS-based tool to help homeless people find a bed for the night. Capabilities may include:

- SMS Bed Finder: the ability to text a zipcode and receive locations of open beds in it.

- SMS Bed Reserver: the ability to text a unique ID and reserve a given bed for the night.

- SMS Bed Cancellation: the ability to cancel a reservation.

- SMS Check-in: the ability to check in to a location to finish "claiming" a bed for the night.

- Web Bed Setup: the ability for care providers to add themselves to the database of available beds.

- Web Bed Update: the ability for care providers to update the status of available beds.

- Web Profile Creation: the abilities to create a profile and assign a unique ID for qualified users.

Now identify the capabilities that are *absolutely required to provide social value.* One way of arriving at this list—a subset of the larger list—is to begin to take things away and see whether the value remains. For example, if you remove the SMS Bed Finder, does the system still achieve the social goals you've set out? Probably not, so that becomes an instrumental capability. Can you take away the Web Profile Creation? Sure—people who want to sign up could work directly with a case manager who could email their information directly to you, and you could set up manual profiles.

The remaining capabilities define the Primary Product Offering. Write these capabilities on a timeline of months, moving from today through 12 months in the future.

Consider which of the removed capabilities would take the least time and effort to add or would add the most value. Add these capabilities to the timeline in a second group, as a Follow-On Product Offering.

Continue adding data points for subsequent feature additions until you've shown how your entire product vision comes to life.

METHODS FOR PLANNING A BUSINESS
PRODUCT AND FEATURE ROADMAP, CONTINUED

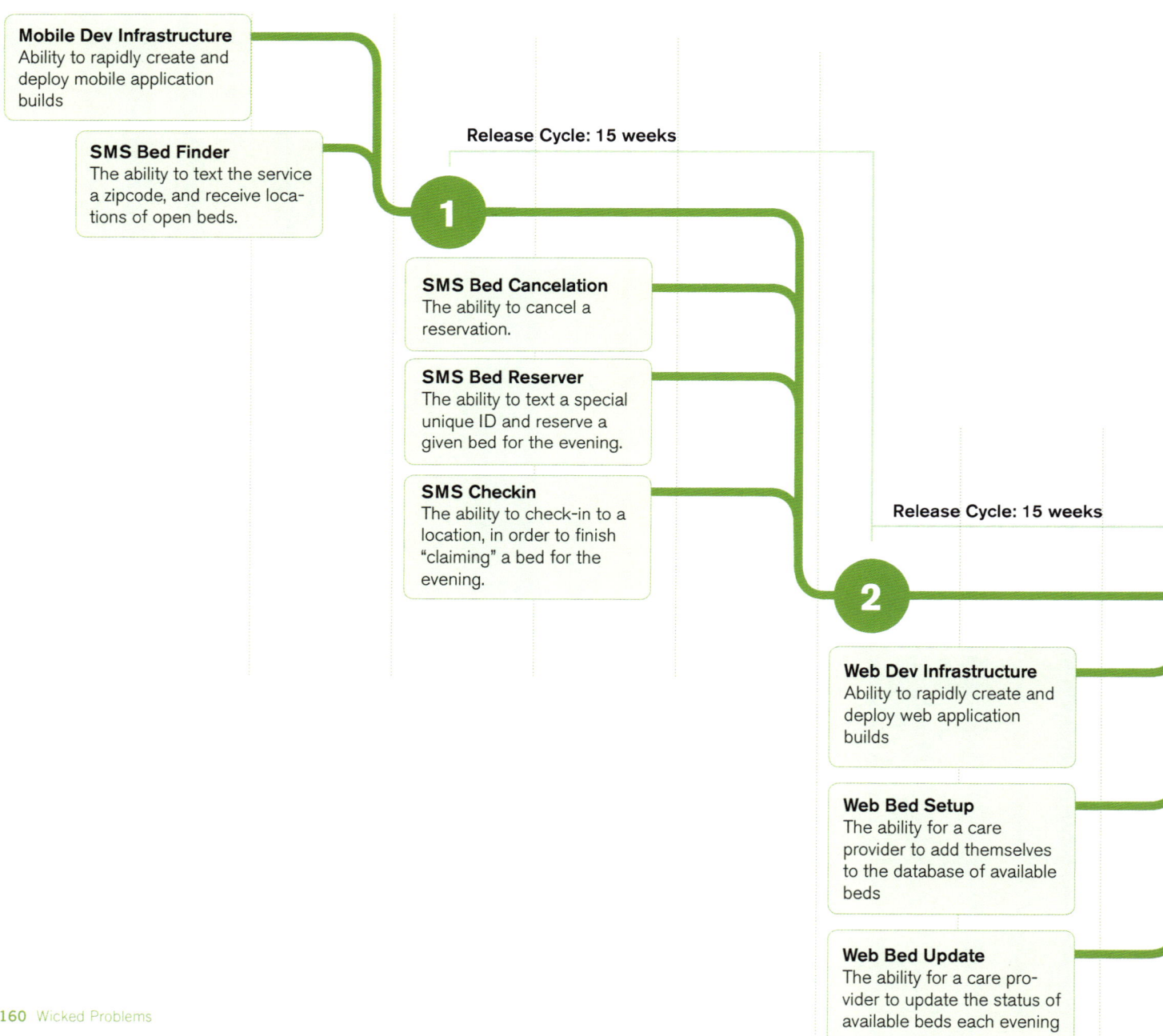

Add dates to the timeline. How fast can you build the product, service, and infrastructure required for your Primary Product Offering? How long will you need to test this in the marketplace before launching the Follow-On Product Offering?

As you ask, and answer, these questions, you'll begin to arrive at a product roadmap—a timeline that describes what you will build, when you will build it, and how long you expect it to take.

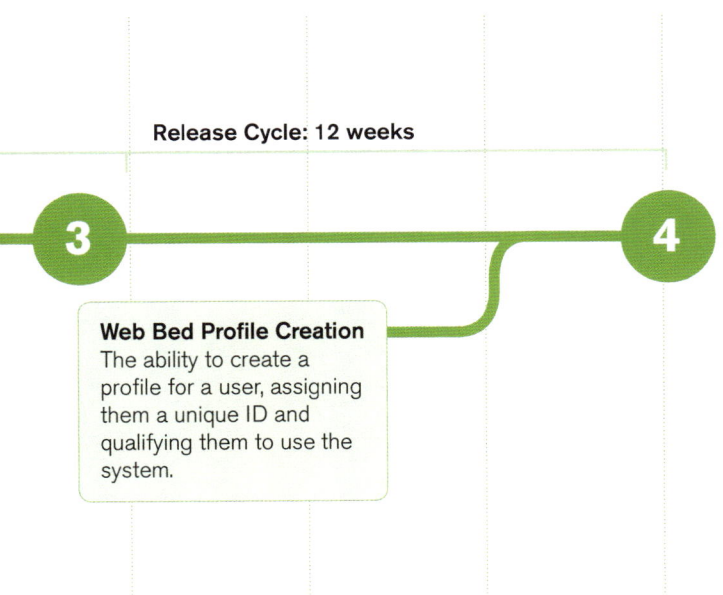

When should I use it?

Create the product and feature roadmap when you have a cohesive idea of what you are making. So it will come after you've created a series of storyboards, described your impact through a Theory of Change model, and modeled your company's finances. Then continue to revise the roadmap as your product grows and changes. You can use the roadmap as a basic program-management tool, to understand how your sales targets and finances relate to your product capabilities. You can also use it to show team members and stakeholders how your product will change over time.

What is the output, and how can I use it?

A product roadmap is a visual timeline. You can use it to drive conversations with your team and with other stakeholders, and to help make decisions and tradeoffs about features.

Learn More

The Wikipedia article on Technology roadmaps provides a useful set of examples and tips for product roadmapping; at https://en.wikipedia.org/wiki/Technology_roadmap

IN
CONCLUSION

Design is powerful. This book has presented a new role for designers, where a designer takes on the responsibilities of a social entrepreneur. This means engaging with wicked problems and using the power of design to generate social capital.

Designers are generally well intentioned. Many designers want to make the world a better place, but feel constrained by existing corporate structures and external expectations. It's my hope that this book offers readers the permission to focus on problems worth solving, and to do the meaningful and important work that our world desperately needs.

WORKS CITED & RECOMMENDED

Amatullo, Mariana, interview by Jon Kolko. (November 16, 2011)

Ashoka. Ashoka - About Us. n.d. http://ashoka.org/facts. (accessed November 14, 2011)

Bauerlein, Mark. The Dumbest Generation: How the Digital Age Stupefies Young Americans and Jeopardizes Our Future. Tarcher, 2009.

Carnegie Mellon University. Integrated Product Development (IPD) course. n.d. http://www.cmu.edu/mpd/capstone-course/index.html (accessed November 14, 2011).

Clark, Hannah. "James Dyson Cleans Up." August 1, 2006. http://www.forbes.com/2006/08/01/leadership-facetime-dyson-cx_hc_0801dyson.html (accessed October 24, 2011)

Cockburn, Alistair. "Use Cases, ten years later." STQE magazine, 2002. http://alistair.cockburn.us/Use+cases,+ten+years+later (accessed October 1, 2011)

Cone, Inc. "The 2006 Cone Millennial Cause Study." 2006.

Coyne, Richard. Logic Models of Design. Pitman, 1988.

Drewnowski, A, and SE Specter. "Poverty and obesity: the role of energy density and energy costs." American Journal of Clinical Nutrition, 2004: 6-16.

Dugger, Celia. "South Africa Is Seen to Lag in H.I.V. Fight." July 20, 2009. http://www.nytimes.com/2009/07/20/world/africa/20circumcision.html (accessed October 1, 2011).

Dyson. "A New Idea." n.d. http://www.dyson.com/about/story/default.asp?searchType=story&story=newidea (accessed October 2011)

Edgington, Nell. "4 Things Every Nonprofit Needs." June 15, 2011. http://www.socialvelocity.net/2011/06/4-things-every-nonprofit-needs/ (accessed November 14, 2011).

Ehn, Pelle. Work-Oriented Design of Computer Artifacts. Stockholm, 1988.

Ford. F150 Detailed Comparison. n.d. http://www.ford.com/trucks/f150/compare/?vehicles=30211|32979|31007|29694 (accessed November 14, 2011).

Foster, Dave. Movirtu and frog design team up to create "telecom cloud." May 21, 2010. http://tech.ashoka.org/movirtu_frog_collaboration (accessed November 14, 2011).

Fukuyama, Francis. "Social Capital and Development: The Coming Agenda." SAIS Review, 2002: 23-37.

Gaver, William, Andrew Boucher, and Sarah Pennington. "Cultural Probes and the Value of Uncertainty." Interactions Magazine, September/October, 2004.

Godin, Seth. "The Problem with Non." September 15, 2009. http://sethgodin.typepad.com/seths_blog/2009/09/the-problem-with-non.html (accessed November 14, 2011).

Grameen Foundation. "Who We Are." n.d. http://www.grameenfoundation.org/who-we-are (accessed November 14, 2011).

Helft, Miguel. "Microsoft Kin Discontinued After 48 Days." June 30, 2010. https://www.nytimes.com/2010/07/01/technology/01phone.html (accessed November 11, 2011).

Jacobs, Jane. The Death and Life of Great American Cities. 1961.

Kumparak, Greg. "It's Official: HP Kills Off webOS Phones and the TouchPad." August 18, 2011. http://techcrunch.com/2011/08/18/its-official-hp-kills-off-webos-phones-and-the-touchpad/ (accessed November 11, 2011).

Marshall, Brigid. Current. November 6, 2008. http://www.odemagazine.com/exchange/3746/the_entitlement_generation_gone_broke (accessed November 14, 2011).

Menger, Ashley, interview by Jon Kolko. Personal Email (November 26, 2011).

Moore, Pat. Disguised: A True Story. 1985.

Novak, Joseph, and Alberto Ca as. "How People Learn." August 29, 2009. http://cmap.ihmc.us/docs/howpeoplelearn.html (accessed November 10, 2011).

Optaros. "It's a Consumer's World. Brands Just Live in It." October 25, 2011. http://www.optaros.com/blogs/its-a-consumers-world-brands-just-live-in-it (accessed November 10, 2011).

Oulasvirta, Antti, Esko Kurvinen, and Tomi Kankainen. "Understanding Contexts by Being There: Case Studies in bodystorming." Pers Ubiquit Comput, 2002: 125-134.

Pavithra Mehta, Suchitra Shenoy. Infinite Vision. CharityFocus, 2011.

Pilloton, Emilly, interview by Jon Kolko. Personal email (November 2, 2011).

WORKS CITED & RECOMMENDED, CONTINUED

RISD. Foundation Studies. n.d. http://www.risd.edu/Academics/Foundation_Studies/ (accessed November 14, 2011).

Rittel, Horst. "Dilemmas in a General Theory of Planning." Policy Sciences, 1973: 155-169.

Sanders, Liz. "Generative Tools for CoDesigning." Collaborative Design, by Ball and Woodcock Scrivener. London: Springer-Verlag London Limited, 2000.

SCAD. Foundation Studies. n.d. http://www.scad.edu/foundation-studies/courses.cfm#programButtons (accessed November 14, 2011).

Schoemaker, Paul. "Scenario Planning: A Tool for Strategic Thinking." Sloan Management Review, no. Winter (1995): 25.

Skoll Foundation. About. n.d. http://www.skollfoundation.org/about/ (accessed November 14, 2011).

Stanford. Design Thinking Bootcamp: Experiences in Innovation and Design. n.d. http://dschool.stanford.edu/classes/#design-thinking-bootcamp-experiences-in-innovation-and-design (accessed November 14, 2011).

Twenge, Jean. Generation Me. Free Press, 2006.

Wikipedia. Canon EOS. n.d. https://secure.wikimedia.org/wikipedia/en/wiki/Canon_EOS (accessed November 11, 2011).

Wikipedia. iPod. n.d. https://secure.wikimedia.org/wikipedia/en/wiki/IPod (accessed November 11, 2011).

Yale School of Management. Project Masiluleke: Texting and Testing to Fight HIV/AIDS in South Africa. n.d. http://nexus.som.yale.edu/design-project-m/ (Accessed November 14, 2011)

Zmuda, Natalie. "Tropicana Line's Sales Plunge 20% Post-Rebranding." April 2, 2009. http://adage.com/article/news/tropicana-line-s-sales-plunge-20-post-rebranding/135735/ (accessed November 10, 2011).

ACKNOWLEDGMENTS

I want to thank the following for their help and support in making this book—and Austin Center for Design—possible:

Thank you to the AC4D advisory board, particularly Carl DiSalvo, Liz Danzico, and Robert Fabricant, for your ongoing support and confidence.

Thank you to my wife Jess Kolko and my parents Ann and Arthur Kolko for believing in my work.

Thank you to my mentor and friend Alec Hazlett for instilling in me a culture of craft and caring.

And thank you to the co-founders of Austin Center for Design—both faculty and alumni—for joining me in this adventure: Professors Lauren Serota, Jon Freach, Justin Petro, and Alumni Scott Magee, Ryan Hubbard, Ruby Ku, Saranyan Vigraham, Christina Tran, Kristine Mudd, Chap Ambrose, Alex Pappas and Kat Davis.

Made in the USA
Charleston, SC
02 December 2012